Mind Control

Mind Control

Mastering the Art of Constructive Influence
or
*How to Get Others to Do What You Want,
and Have Them Think It Was Their Idea!*

In Mind Control Dr. William Horton, Psy. D. takes us closer to the practical
application "Mind Control" a term filled with mystery, intrigue and fun.
Can you imagine your life in a world where people simply do what you ask
them to do? The process outlined in this book will install the skills needed
for maximum success. Control of the mind is here!

Scott McFall, DCH Founder: Dakota Hypnosis Motivation Clinics

William Horton, Psy. D.

To order additional copies of this book, contact:
Xlibris Corporation
1-888-795-4274
www.Xlibris.com
Orders@Xlibris.com
35275

CONTENTS

If NLP is something that you thirst to use and apply in business, or in everyday life, then you want to pick up *Mind Control* today! Wil Horton collects a treasure trove of NLP techniques and strategies designed to influence and persuade others into one easy-to-read text. Where else are you going to get this many practical applications for this little investment. Get it today!

—Richard Alexander,
Master Hypnotist, NLP Trainer

==================

It was a summer afternoon in Chicago. 1995. Across from me was Dr. William Horton, Psy. D.. We talked NLP, influence, everything there was to talk about motivating others to do things they need to be doing in life. Ten years later after having taken two divergent paths to teach others how to persuade and how to master the art of mind control, we meet again here, in Dr. Horton's new book on Mind Control. His desire for all techniques and strategies to be used to help people be better, be happier, be healthier shines through a vast array of tools you can use to influence others.

You'll learn how to anchor resourceful states in others, build rapport, and even get a list of Dr. Horton's "bypass words." I'll save that surprise for you.

Where else are you going to get all of the NLP techniques designed to influence others crystallized into one workable tome? They are here. NLP'ers in particular will enjoy this journey because it will be like coming home.

What Dr. Horton does so well is make some of the more seemingly complex elements of NLP easy to understand and far more importantly apply.

Enjoy your journey and take this book with you on all of yours.

The only problem I have with this book is I wish I would have written it!

—Kevin Hogan, author of *The Science of Influence* and *The Psychology of Persuasion*

PROLOGUE

"Mind control" a term filled with mystery, intrigue, and fun. Control of the mind . . . what does it mean, really! So-called experts have been writing and arguing about the mind for as long as people have been able to communicate.

The elusive and mystical control we seek is possible. In *Mind Control*, Dr. William Horton, Psy. D. takes us closer to the practical application of mental discipline for ourselves. Dr. Horton applies NLP communication techniques (special language to structure change in the mind) so that we can manage and control of others. This control takes the form of better understanding of what we see feel and hear as other talk to us. We are afforded the opportunity through these techniques to use the best possible angle while talking with others.

In our culture, control can be regarded as a negative term. Here we use it as a positive action. When we say control, we really refer to the control of our own thoughts, our own state of mind, and the way we communicate.

Dr. Horton uses his ability to break down systems and processes to share a new understanding of the function of the mind as we interact with the people around us. Can you imagine your life in a world where people simply do what you ask them to do? The processes outlined in this book will install the skills needed for maximum success.

Self-control and mental discipline give you the ability to have more success in any part of your journey through career and personal goals. Personal relationships become more rewarding. You have an easy time controlling money. Your ability to retain information grows. This is all possible because you are choosing the way you communicate with yourself and the other players in your life.

Imagine a life where you control your emotional reactions to the obstacles you encounter on your path to success. See yourself as an individual who can consider the effects your reactions have on others. Hear your own thoughts as they become useful to your goals. You can have all of this and more. All you must do is master the techniques in this book.

Even more exciting news awaits you. With the techniques you learn, you can enable others to reach their dreams and goals in a more effective manner. It's easy to remember times in your life when you wanted other people to simply do what you have asked them to do. What if you knew exactly how to talk and act to get others to take action? The more you understand "mind control," the easier your interactions with other people become.

As you remember each technique in this book, you will enjoy Dr. Horton's unique take on the material and his passion for life itself.

—Elsom Eldrige, author of "*The Obvious Expert*",
Founder of The International Guild of Professional Consultants.

AUTHORS NOTE

As I read the edited manuscript for this book, I am reminded that I am one of the luckiest men in the world. A little over 20 years ago I was exposed to the technology in this book and it not only saved my life it gave me a life worth living. I was caught in a cycle of addiction and self destruction that I, with my limited thought processes could not escape. I have done nothing special to have the opportunity to live the life I currently have. I have a beautiful home, a beautiful wife, a successful daughter, and I have had more success financially in one month than I thought possible.

I just returned from a trip to Asia teaching the techniques outlined in this book. The idea that a man who at one point was living in a run down trailer and could not stop drinking and other self destructive behaviors in a relatively short period of time become a licensed psychologist, author and world traveled speaker on Hypnosis, NLP and Mind Control boggles my mind and fills me with a gratitude I can never repay. The magic does not stop there, these techniques have also allowed me to overcome a severe physical injury where I was told I would always have a limp and my athletic days were over, would become a 4th degree black belt in karate and have won tournaments and medals in various competitions. Today I ran a 8:45 mile, not bad for someone told they could never do this!

None of this would have been possible without the techniques I have outlined in this book. I pray that you read and take in the information and that you use it to live the life you deserve. It is one of my primary missions to share this information with as many people as I can. I have taught thousands of students and always learn new things, I know that you too will one day be able to share with me new and wonderful applications of the technology you are about to learn.

I hope to see you on the road to happy destiny!

William Horton, Psy. D. CAC CMI

CHAPTER 1

An Introduction to Mind Control

The human mind is a remarkable thing. But we often take it for granted. We do not give it the full respect it deserves. I guess this is largely because it is capable of taking care of itself. It usually doesn't demand any attention from us, so we don't give it any. But what if we did? What if we stopped for a minute or two and thought about the range of activities going on in the human mind, and the amazing faculties that our minds have?

Only a reflection along these lines helps us understand what a wonderful entity the human mind is. Our minds are capable of carrying out so many routine activities, like thinking, feeling, remembering, calculating, analyzing, and reasoning. Oh! The list could go on and on and on. Apart from this, we are also capable of doing so many other things totally alien to the rest of creation. For example, we can enjoy music, appreciate beauty, create beautiful things, and so on, that only humans are capable of doing.

Isn't it these finer qualities that distinguish man from beast? And all this is, of course, thanks to the human mind all of us have been endowed with. But then, if the human mind is capable of such an astounding range of qualities, it makes one wonder whether its potential has actually been tapped. Forget about tapping it to the fullest possible extent; do we use even a third of the potential that our minds have?

Pondering a question like this opens up another avenue of thought: If the human mind is capable of so many activities and functions, if the human mind is so powerful, can't this power be used to exercise some degree of power over other human minds?

It seems logical enough, doesn't it? Most of us do not use even a fraction of our mind's faculties. So if some of us start doing that, if we start directing and focusing our mental energy toward the minds of others—which, mind you, function in very similar patterns as our mind—can't we exercise a sort of mind control over them?

If this concept interests you, then you can very well put your best foot forward, for this book is completely dedicated to the use and development of mind power. Believe me, you will be surprised at the amount of power you can exercise over others!

Now hold on a second—we are not talking about looking at the guy standing across the street and being able to control his mind to such an extent that he turns toward you and starts waving his hand. That kind of thing only happens in comics, cartoons, and movies!

We are talking about something more practical. We are talking about using mind power so you can talk convincingly to a person and effectively bring that person to your line of thinking. Who would want to do that, you might wonder. Well, a lot of people would indeed love to do just that—and succeed!

Take for instance a single day in your life. How many people do you meet in a day? Out of that, how many of them do you talk to? You may not be a salesman, but trust me when I tell you all of us try to do a lot of marketing in the course of our daily life.

We try to sell our ideas; we try to sell our thoughts, our feelings, our desires, our likes and our dislikes. When two people meet and start talking, there is always bound to be an exchange of different views. So how do we get others to accept our views? How do we sell our opinions? How do we bring others to accept our ideas?

Mind you, the people I am talking about need not necessarily be strangers. They can be members of your immediate family—your parents, your kids, your spouse, your siblings, or they could be your teachers, your friends, or your neighbors. They could also be people you do daily business with, like the postman, or the grocer, or the shopkeeper, or the maid, even your colleagues or your boss.

All these transactions give rise to situations that may end in one of three ways:

- The "win-lose" situation, in which one party wins and the other party loses.
- The "lose-lose" situation, in which neither party wins—it is just like a tug-of-war in which both parties hold on strongly to their views and together they get nowhere.
- And finally, there is the "win-win" situation, in which both parties are convinced that each got the best out of the situation.

Let's discuss the situation in which one party eventually wins. The other party in effect loses, but when the two part ways, the second party leaves with the conviction that he or she won the struggle.

That is precisely what mind power is all about—you use your mental faculties to get the better of others, but they are unaware of the end result. They beat a graceful retreat and actually feel good about it, so much so that though you got your way, they believe they got theirs!

This is a technique worth learning. It will be of immense help to you in tackling the different situations you face in life. After all, how many times in life have others got the better of us? How many times in life have we had to negotiate and had to leave feeling that we got raw deals?

In the course of this program we will learn how to use the techniques of neuro-psychogenics and neurolinguistic programming (NLP) to develop mind control. But before we really hit the road, here's an eye-opener about NLP.

What Is NLP?

NLP is "neurolinguistic programming." A unique model of how people learn, motivate themselves, and change their behavior to achieve excellence in any endeavor, the term NLP was coined by (author and founder of general semantics) Alfred Habdank Skarbek Korzybski. Richard Bandler and John Grinder brought it to the public. From their trainings this science has grown. They are to be commended on advancing this art and science.

NLP is an integration of neurology, psychology, linguistics, cybernetics, and systems theory:

- **Neuro**—because our experiences, both conscious and subconscious, are derived through and from our senses and central nervous system.
- **Linguistic**—because our mental processes are also coded, organized, given meaning and transformed through language.
- **Programming**—because people interact as a system in which experience and communication is composed of sequences of patterns or "programs."

The functions of NLP include letting you model or copy human excellence and helping you become adept at whatever you want to do.

NLP helps you become a better communicator in terms of:

- Business consultation
- Parenting
- Management
- Nursing
- Negotiation
- Public Speaking
- Education
- Sports Performance
- Counseling
- Therapy
- Relationships

NLP can:

- change past impact on a client
- turn a poor speller to a good speller
- assist a business person to gain rapport nonverbally and handle meetings efficiently
- help an athlete improve concentration

- be used as a method of therapy
- can serve as a process of teaching people to use their brains

Most therapy is remedial, i.e., directed toward solving problems of the past. NLP studies excellence and teaches skills that promote positive changes, which in turn generate new possibilities and opportunities.

This program is designed to equip you with all that you need to become a master of mind power. Written in a very simple, lucid style, with no stone left unturned in terms of rendering all scientific jargon in layman's lingo, this book can even help a beginner become a master in no time! That said, let us now proceed to the first step toward exercising mind control.

The first step is to open your senses; you will be only as good as the information you allow in. We want you to allow more information to enter into your awareness. The first step is to practice opening your senses. Try the following.

Sensory Acuity Exercises

Kinesthetic (Sense of Touch)

First, find your center for the sense of feeling. You need to get in touch with a time where you were really in tune with your body during a physical activity, such as working out, dancing, sports, etc. The focus should be on your feeling center. Now you should take several items and feel them. Normal everyday items, an apple, a pencil, a newspaper, some cloth. Get into the feeling of the experience of touching it. Now close your eyes and repeat it. Imagine expanding your sense of touch so you are ten times more sensitive. Now stay in your center and think of some physical states of feeling, Happy, sad, energetic, depressed, etc. Repeat the above and see how it alters your experience. Now go through a day and stay focused on your sense of touch/feeling.

Auditory

First, you will focus on your center of hearing. Think of a time when they were really in tune with your sense of hearing, such as listening to music, the sounds of nature, etc. Now keep your focus on this auditory center as you listen to sounds. Do this in several places. At home, listen for the background sounds you normally screen out, fans, air-conditioning, TV in another room. Notice how you can expand your hearing. Now do this in a public place and do the same; notice you can hear others' conversations.

Now listen closely listen in your conversations. Notice if your hear more, listen for inflections, tone, pace rhythm. Really listen to the people you normally screen out. Spend the day expanding your hearing; you will be surprised!

Visual

Now you will focus on your center for the sense of vision. Think of a time when you were visually in tune with their body (at a movie, looking at a painting, etc.). Now look at several items and imagine your vision expanding. Notice all the little things. Watch a movie or TV show, and watch the sides, not just the center. Notice how it may change your experience of the film. Watch a movie you like and force yourself to do this. (We naturally are drawn to the center) Then focus on what you see when you are talking to someone. See how it changes your communications. Now you will then focus approximately three to four feet behind the person you are conversing with.

CHAPTER 2

The Brain and the Mind

The brain and the mind have different jobs. In order to understand how "mind control" works, you need to understand what is occurring inside your head (and your subject's head) as you use NLP to achieve the best results possible.

The Brain

The brain is a tangible thing. You know where it is, roughly what it looks like, and what it's made of. It has properties that dictate how it functions, and we know what those properties are. One of them, the one that is most important for mind control, is subconscious communication.

The level that our brain is operating in dictates how we feel, how we behave, and how we perform. The mind control state is attained by taking your brain from beta, which it is probably in right now, to either the alpha or theta states, depending on what you want to achieve. There has been a lot of research into the four levels of brain activity, beta, alpha, theta, and delta.

Beta state is the home to logic, analysis, and reason. You are awake, alert, in a normal state of consciousness. You are experiencing sight, sound, smell, taste, and touch. Beta state only makes up approximately 12 percent of your total conscious being. It significantly affects the brain's ability to store information and memories, access creativity, focus, and concentration. We spend about 90 percent of our day stuck in this state, which isn't any surprise that it's also where we get most of our tension and negative thinking.

Alpha state is the strongest and most prominent brain state. It's also the best state to be in when preparing for competition and for decision making. Alpha state is a state of calm, relaxation, and lucidity. You must be in alpha state to modify, add, and delete "programs" for behavior modification. You can also control dreams while in this state. Alpha state is where you are in the approximate twenty minutes or so while you are falling, but not quite, asleep.

Theta state is where you end up after leaving alpha state when you fall asleep, but before you are sleeping deeply. This is the state of active dreaming and rapid eye movement activity. It's also the level you can reach when you are hypnotized by someone else, and where deep programming can take place. It is a state of deep relaxation and clear mental imagery.

Delta state is the deepest state of deep, dreamless sleep. This is where healing and recovery in the body and brain can take place. The body is completely at rest.

The Mind

Think of yourself as having basically two minds: your conscious mind and your subconscious mind. Your conscious mind is your thinking, awake state of awareness, yet it comprises a remarkably paltry 12 percent of your mind. Mind control happens when you bypass the 12 percent conscious mind and get to the power center. But first, let's review.

Your conscious mind has five functions:

1. Analysis
2. Rationalization
3. Willpower
4. Functional memory
5. Voluntary body functions

1. Analysis: Your conscious mind is logical because it is analytical. Its job is to study problems that you have and solve them. This is the place where people try to influence with logical reasoning. True mind control experts understand this is the least effective use of influence.
2. Rationalization: This part of your mind tells you why you do things, gives you reasons to do things, helps you understand. Problem is, it's usually wrong, because true motivation for behavior and responses comes from a much deeper part of our mind that we don't normally have access to with our conscious mind. Think of smokers—they might say they smoke because it relaxes them. That's not really why, but it's the rationalization their brain told them, and it's a tidy, neat, logical answer. Not complete and certainly not correct, but logical.
3. Willpower: This is what makes you stop and think before doing something. Problem is, the conscious mind really isn't very good at this function. (If it were, there would be a lot of therapists, counselors, and hypnotists out of jobs!)
4. Functional Memory: The short-term memory, our functioning memory, is usually all you need to get through life. That's why even though in third grade you needed to know how to get from your classroom to the bathroom, decades later you can't even remember where your third grade classroom was. The brain drops (but doesn't totally "lose") the stuff that we don't need to survive on a day-to-day basis.

5. Voluntary Body Functions: As long as you aren't physically impaired by injury, illness, or other physical condition, your brain tells your legs, "Hey, let's go," or tells your hand to keep away from that hot stove. But if you tried to control your internal bodily functions that are normally on autopilot—like digestion and blood pressure—unless you've been trained to do this, normally you cannot unless you access them through some form of hypnosis.

Remember, your conscious mind makes up approximately 12 percent of your entire mind. That's not a lot! So somewhere else, there must be some pretty exciting stuff going on that we need to learn how to communicate with.

The key to mind control is the subconscious mind. That 88 percent of your mind is the power center; it's the motherboard of your body. Just like with a computer, as long as it's working properly, you never know it's there. But if it wasn't there, nothing else could happen. Its single most significant characteristic is that it literally runs your life without you knowing it. The problem is that many people spend too much time listening to that loud and obnoxious 12 percent instead of tapping into the true power center. Like an iceberg, the subconscious is hidden beneath deep, dark waters, with only a small part showing on the surface.

Our mind was meant to function differently, but we don't understand it. We're like a monkey pounding away on a keyboard with no comprehension as to how the computer works. Sometimes the monkey gets lucky and something good happens. And of the people who do know how to tap into the subconscious, many have made it a point to appear to be a huge, mystical deal that takes years of patience to master. The truth is, it's just a matter of knowing the way to activate it.

The key to mind control is simple:

- **The subconscious mind cannot think, reason, or argue.** So what does it do? It FEELS.
- **The subconscious mind is the emotional center of your being.** Control someone's emotions, and you control THEM. And many times, your emotions are actually out of sight, buried beneath your conscious mind or disguised by the rationalization.
- **Your subconscious mind controls who you are, how you respond, and what you believe.** You (usually) don't stop and think about your beliefs when you respond to a situation. But your responses are usually based upon your belief system.
- **Your habits are a function of your subconscious mind.** When you repeat the same action over and over, eventually it will become a habit. A habit is an automatic response. It is an action that starts in the conscious mind and, through repetition, shifts into the realm of the subconscious, like using a turn signal (for some of us).
- **The subconscious mind is a huge storage unit for all memories, thoughts, dreams, fantasies, and experiences, whether real or imagined.** The

subconscious simply records everything; it doesn't make judgments as to the reality of it.

- **The subconscious protects you from real and imagined dangers.** This is good to keep you safe, but bad because it's how phobias take root.

The conscious and subconscious minds work together. Your subconscious mind holds all your long-term memories, and while it influences how your conscious mind works and acts, it can be programmed (or reprogrammed) to do what you want it to do.

The conscious mind is the active master; it shows the effect of who you are, thinks, perceives, exerts will and is aware, instigates activity, and can be objective.

The subconscious mind is like a servant but is the cause of who you are, controls your feelings, blindly records your experiences and thoughts, is the source of your personal power, and is totally subjective.

Mind control is about taking control of the subconscious mind. This is very powerful, because if a suggestion is allowed to travel from your conscious to your subconscious mind, then it has the power to change your beliefs and behaviors.

But first, a suggestion has to make it through the critical factor of the conscious mind. That is the part of the conscious mind that works to protect the status quo of your subconscious mind. It's the part of you that keeps you from believing every single thing you are told and getting manipulated. It acts as a filter to make sure what you are hearing is in agreement with what's already stored.

Political and religious debates really bring critical factor to the forefront. But how can you break through that filter to get through to the subconscious mind?

Mind control bypasses the critical factor of the conscious mind to allow you to access the subconscious and focus the mind to accept new positive information such as suggestions.

Now, if that was all there was to mind control, we would be able to control others, but that's not the case. We need to use several tools to bypass the critical factor and obtain the success we want.

A great example of this was in the 2004 presidential election. President Bush and the Republicans constantly used the term "September 11" or "9-11 changed everything."

I remember a question about education and how to fund college scholarships; without missing a beat the vice president replied, "Well we have to remember 9-11 changed the world; we have to defeat the terrorists, and there are bad people who want to kill us. The Democrats would rather talk to them and find out why they hate us," he then answered something about education, but why mention 9-11 and terrorists?

FEAR! It elicits a state; then he can link it to whatever he wants. This is a great use of bypassing the critical factors and moving people. Start to look for examples of this in the real world!

CHAPTER 3

Rapport: The First Key

We start with the relatively simple concept of *rapport*. Put simply, establishing rapport is getting a person to trust you. Is that important? you ask. Of course it is. Let's take a look at the situation this way. Go back in time, maybe the prehistoric era, when cavemen roamed the earth. If you could conjure up images of the Flintstones, it certainly would help to get a clearer picture of what I am talking about.

In those days, survival was indeed a very crucial issue. With the threats from wild animals on the one hand, and the forces of nature on the other, it was survival of the fittest! That apart, there was also a lot of fear arising from the existence of other cavemen. Man had not yet become a social animal, and there was a lot of hostility among the cavemen. Each caveman regarded another as a threat to his own survival—his food, his domain, and yes, his mate, too! Of course, they had not yet begun living together, and so the first instinct was to attack one another.

When two cavemen met, it was a question of who should attack and kill first. Killing meant the survival of the killer. They didn't have an established language; their speech probably consisted mostly of grunts and sounds. But gradually they started accepting the fact that they could be friends and that there was safety in numbers. But how could each know whether the other caveman they met was hostile or friendly?

It's quite easy to picture the scene. Caveman Ugg is on his way to the local caveman shopping mall (looking out for a beast to clobber for dinner), when all at once he comes across this other caveman, Caveman Ogg. They spot each other and freeze. They eye each other from a distance. Ugg is dressed in deerskin while Ogg is dressed in bearskin—clearly signs of different cultures!

As they advance, their hearts race. Each one suspects the other's motives and wonders if the other is going to attack. Apparently, neither wants to start the fight that could end in loss of life. Once they come within a safe distance, they start circling each other like they have seen animals do. They scan each other for signs of weapons. Each one has a sharp flint in his hand.

After a while of circling, there is no sign of attack. So what do they do? Both decide that there is not much danger. And then in an instant, they both drop their weapons and advance toward each other with exposed palms indicating they are unarmed.

This process of building trust, when each party feels there is no threat from the other, is what's called building rapport—a concept that came into existence during the time of the cavemen and continues to this very day.

Of course, today's conditions are very different and we usually don't start attacking strangers we meet on the way to work. But one thing is still the same: we still do not trust most of the people we confront! Maybe distrust was handed down by cavemen, or maybe it's because there are just too many con men and swindlers walking around today.

Whatever the reason, trust is not something that comes easily. The funny thing is we are more likely to trust a person who has been introduced to us by a common friend than a person we meet directly. This process of trust building is rapport. And before we go on, just a reminder: the 't' in rapport is silent—the word is pronounced "rappor." Got it?

Establishing Rapport

When we talk about "mind control" we must understand the importance of rapport. Rapport is the first and most important step toward building a relationship. Unlike the cavemen, we do not walk about with weapons we can throw down to show others we mean them no harm. We have to use more subtle ways to convince them of this. Rapport in modern terms means meeting people on their terms, not ours. This is where you establish trust and credibility.

To do this, you must first be able to meet people on their terms, because people tend to have the "What's in it for me?" idea running in the background. This is a mistake that most of us make. We always try to judge others by our level of thinking when it is much easier to use to their level of thinking. Most people are driven by profit motives, profit meaning not just money, but benefit to themselves, their family, etc. So all you have to do is convince them that not only do they have nothing to lose from this transaction, but that, on the contrary, they have a lot to gain.

At first glance this might seem very difficult, because how do you convince a person that they have a lot to gain from a relationship with you when apparently you don't have much to offer? The secret to remember is you don't really have to give the person something in terms of material goods.

There is a lot more that a person can offer. You can call it the dynamics of social relationships if you wish. You can give a person a lot without parting with your material goods and money. As a matter of fact, people are looking for people like you who have a lot to offer. Give it to them, and you will have them eating out of your hand. And here's how to do it. We all know that a lot of, if not most, communication takes place in a nonverbal manner, so why not use this? You don't really have to even open your mouth and speak to get an idea across. You can depend on body language to do it for you.

How many times have you heard it's not just what you say but how you say it that matters? Keep this in mind and you will find things are a whole lot easier. You should also remember that from now on you are moving toward becoming an expert communicator. Whatever you are doing is now no longer the product of the unconscious; rather, you are working on the conscious level.

The other person, by contrast, is not fully aware of what's happening, and you are working on their unconscious mind. The person will then have no idea what hit them, and before the person can actually think of what happened, you will have got your wish fulfilled.

As a matter of fact, you have been "mirroring" all your life. This is how you learned as a child. You learned verbal communication by going through three stages, babbling, mirroring, and echolalia. You AUTOMATICALLY will mirror anyone you have a rapport with. This does not really come out of a conscious effort but is rather spontaneous.

Rapport Key: People like others who are like them.

This does not necessarily mean there should be a physical similarity between two people. It can have the same effect if two people are in fact doing the same things like standing or sitting in the same positions, assuming the same postures and talking about a topic on which they mutually agree.

- Have you ever yawned because someone else yawned?
- When a friend stubs his toe, do you flinch and make the same type of face?
- Have you ever looked up because others were looking up?
- Have you ever started itching because you watched someone else itch?
- Have you ever ended up picking up a Southern accent because you were talking to someone from the south a tad too long?

The most basic level of rapport is physically mirroring the person you are targeting.

When you mirror someone you are simply offering that person a reflection of himself or herself. This simple technique has a super powerful impact, because of the way people respond to their own behavior. It is quite remarkable how people take a cue from somebody who apparently is trying to imitate them. There is an old saying that goes, "Imitation is the best kind of flattery." How true that really is! All of us seek approval and appreciation, and what better way to show appreciation than to try and do and act like the other person is doing or saying.

When you offer back to your target their own behavior, they relate to it on a subconscious level and experience a sense of unity. There is little in life as satisfying as seeing a reflection of our selves in another. This is one of the most powerful tools in Mind control.

When you see a couple of friends at a coffee shop in conversation, chances are you will find them sitting in the same position and making the same movements and gestures. If you are in a relationship (and you are getting along), you will notice how you and your partner are sitting in the same physical position if you are in close proximity with each other. You will also breathe with them.

In physics there is a law called "entrainment" which states that if two items in motion are in close enough proximity, they will synchronize. If you put two grandfather clocks in the same room, their pendulums will eventually swing together. This seems to also work for living creatures.

I remember being in New York City teaching this concept, and during a break I had a few of the students look around the room where we were drinking coffee. You could plainly see that the people engaged in conversation were sitting there mirroring and matching each other to the point of having nearly all the same gestures and movements. They had only known each other for a few hours and yet had established a common bond (learning mind control techniques), thereby establishing a very natural rapport with each other. Later that day while walking to dinner with several of the students, we saw several examples of this natural occurrence:

- Two NYPD officers talking at a coffee shop, both leaning against the wall, gesturing with the hand not holding coffee.
- A couple in love on a park bench in intimate conversation, their movements perfectly synchronized.
- Two cab drivers in a very loud, animated conversation on directions to an address.

Since this happens in nature, let's speed up this phenomenon.

What you want to do is present to your target's subconscious mind a mirror image of themselves. This puts your target at ease at a subconscious level, since rapport is natural in friendship, and it speeds up this process. You want to first match physically your target's stance. You assume the same position as they are, sitting the same way, or standing the same way.

- Breathe at the same rate as they do.
- If they lean slightly, you lean the same way.
- If they cross their legs, you cross yours.
- If they adjust their clothes in some way, you adjust yours in like manner.

But you have to be careful about something very important: your targets must not feel that you are trying to consciously mimic them and are in any way making fun of them. So how can you do this without making it too obvious?

That's easy! Try this:

1. Slow down your responses by about one to three seconds.
2. Keep your focus on your target; never mind if the movement is not natural to you. If your target does it, you do it. If you are focused on how you feel, you are not focused on your target. Your internal state is not important—only the goal of establishing rapport.

Try this as an experiment: the next time you are in a conversation with someone and you feel there's a rapport, lean against a wall or lean back and continue talking. Watch what happens. A few seconds later the other person will lean as well. Then cross your arms . . . the other will follow suit.

The more you are in rapport, the more mirroring and matching will occur. Once you are in complete rapport, you are in position to persuade the other to do as you wish.

A word of caution!

Now that you are aware of this powerful tool, you will begin to understand why it is so important that you be careful and aware of the messages you are transmitting to your target nonverbally! If you are in rapport, the people you are communicating with will mirror your:

- Frustration
- Hatred
- Anger
- Disbelief (in them, yourself, or a product)

I stress this because we see this all the time. In fact, historically, leaders have taken societies to war by having the populace mirror their feelings. This, of course, can happen very subtly. Once while teaching a class, I received some bad news, and even though I tried to not let my anger show, the class suddenly took on a very negative tone. The students were mirroring my internal state. I had spent a great deal of time getting into rapport with the class, and now it was coming right back at me. It renewed my respect for this technology which indicates that people will mirror their environment.

Exercises to Master Rapport

Breathing:

Mirroring someone's breathing is subtle because breathing itself is such an extremely subconscious process. When you mirror and match another person this way it is almost impossible to detect, because it is something we all have to do.

Pick some targets (people) to match breathing with, in:

- A coffee shop
- A business meeting
- A party

Physical Posture:

As stated before when people are in rapport, they mirror each other. When you do this consciously, you move into the area of gaining trust and confidence at will.

To achieve this you must practice being able to mirror and match others at will. The following steps will help you to get the hang of it.

1. Start in an easy place—your workplace preferably.
2. Pick and choose people you know rather well and mirror and match them in a conversation—you are doing this anyway, but now move into the conscious level.
3. Pick a coworker you know the least and start a conversation, physically mirror and match the other person, maintain your focus on him/her.
4. Start a conversation with your boss and do the same.

Note: Stay away from controversial subjects at this level.

Now you are ready to move into a social setting.

Start a conversation with someone in a coffee shop or restaurant, using the mirror and match technique.

Special Bonus: Remote Rapport Targeting

To prove the power of this technology, go to a public place again, like, say, a coffee shop, and pick a target. Once you have the target spotted, get into the other's peripheral vision (off to the side) and begin to mirror and match from a distance. This is especially fun at a coffee shop. Sit the way the other does. Breathe with the other. The other takes a sip; you take a sip (have the same kind of drink, if possible). You will be amazed at how, before long, your target will start a conversation with you. He/she will be drawn to you.

The following story will illustrate the efficacy of this technique:

I was driving down from Chicago to Florida to teach an advanced mind control class. On the way, I decided to test my "targeting" skills. So I stopped at a Waffle House at about midnight. I picked a person sitting at the counter. He was not like me at all physically—a big man (belly way over belt!), with long hair pulled back into a ponytail and a full beard, a leather vest, and a trucker's wallet (the type with a chain to the belt). I am short, in shape, short haired, and clean shaven, and I was wearing dress slacks and a sport shirt. Opposites if you will!

After sitting for a while, I assumed the same physical posture as my target. I noticed my target was reading a paper while he ate and drank his coffee. I had a magazine, so I pretended to be reading it. He turned a page; I did also. If he took a bite of food, I would. He took a drink of coffee; of course I did too.

He refilled his coffee, so I got the waitress to refill my cup. About this time he started a conversation. He asked who I drove for (he assumed I too was a trucker). I just said I was on my way to a seminar. He looked at my reading material and asked if it was a martial arts seminar. I just nodded; as we talked I kept the focus on him and on what he wanted from life.

Now, I knew I needed to test the level of rapport. As we talked more, my target stated that after this cup he was going to pull out and get back on the road. As he drank his coffee, every time he took a sip, I would also, only a very small sip. When his cup was empty, mine was still half full. I picked up my coffee and, taking a deep gulp, said it was good and that I would have one more.

My target looked around, looked at his watch, and said, "I think I will have one more, too—have to drive late anyway! Could use the coffee." He was in rapport and wanted to stay that way, so his conscious mind rationalized why he would stay (maybe this is why it is hard to get out of a bar with friends!).

Before our conversation was over, he told me all of his personal problems, including a prostrate problem that caused sexual dysfunction. I state this because guys do not talk about this difficulty easily, except with close friends, even then, rarely. He stated it as if he knew me for years. When I suggested he see a hypnotist, he answered he would. This again reminded me of the power of this technology.

Amazed? Practice these skills—and see how much more you will be amazed!

CHAPTER 4

The Second Key
Communication Styles

The goal here is to learn how your target thinks!

Now that you know how to get into a subconscious rapport with someone, you need to know the secret to decode their thoughts. When you begin to think about how people think, the process of how your mind works really becomes important. Many of us start to think about all the things psychology has taught us in recent years. Unconscious motives, and the theories Freud, Jung, and all the other great psychological minds have come up with in the last one hundred years come to our mind.

I know all of this is great information, but it is of little use to any of us who want to quickly influence people with our way of thinking (and acting). What you want is a quick way to decode what is going on in your target's head. Right? Well, the process of discerning that is what is called "neuro-psychogenics." We want to know, quickly, how a person's mind is processing information. As for the why, which constitutes the deep psychological theories, we shall leave that to the researchers!

I have hypnotized well over seventy-five thousand people, fifty thousand of those in the last three years. While I was doing this, I researched what worked in the real world. What I found was startling: people think in very simple ways. This is not to say people are simple—no! We are not! We each have a complex psychological makeup that affords us options relative to how we respond to the world, but how we really think is rather simple.

What I am stating is that the way people process information is very basic. You have five senses, visual, auditory, kinesthetic (feeling), olfactory (smell), and gustatory (taste). These are your only senses, and this is what your brain uses to process information. It is logical to project that this is how people will also process information. So this is how you think.

Most of the people you will ever deal with process information primarily in one of three ways:

1. **Visual (seeing)**
2. **Auditory (hearing)**
3. **Kinesthetic (feeling)**

We use all of these to communicate, but there is usually a predominant way a person likes to communicate (and think). If you know how your target thinks and communicates, it puts you into a deeper level of rapport, thus causing the other to open up to your influence, i.e., to your way of thinking.

I would bet if you monitor most of your friends, especially your closest friends, you would find you use the same communication styles. This is natural. You do not have to work at communicating with them—you're already on the same wavelength. It sounds good to all of you, or it just feels right talking to them.

See if any of the following apply to you, or to someone you know:

Visual people are those who:

- Speak fast (remember a picture is worth a thousand words!) they also use broken sentences and may jump ahead and finish your statements.
- Gesture a lot with their hands. Use a lot of pointed movements.
- Breathe shallow and fast; they may even get breathless if speaking on a subject they like.
- Are very mindful of how they look—colorful, and like to match (would rather look good than be comfortable!).
- Look up a lot with their eyes.
- Socialize a lot—like being seen in the right places at the right time!
- Are neat freaks.
- Are impatient.
- Are result-oriented—get the job done.
- Use SHOW ME as their watch words!
- Think very fast (speed of light versus speed of sound).
- Love graphs, charts, visual presentations, EYE CANDY.
- Like short clear, concise presentations that get to the point.
- Hate being interrupted—they may lose their thoughts.
- Ask questions that stimulate visual responses—"How will this look to the others?"
- Are keen on: "Can you see this happening? Would you like to see our information?"
- Use visual words: *look, see clear, sharp, focus.*

Auditory people:

- Speak slower and are rhythmic.
- Like long conversations.

- Tug at their ears or touch their mouth.
- Have deeper breathing, midchest range.
- Are more casual in dress—no bright colors, but still like to "match"!
- Are slower in their thought process but are more deliberate in their thinking.
- Like to talk things over with others as well as with themselves to check on how it sounds.
- Love animals, have a kinship with nature.
- Look to the sides a lot.
- Would rather live in the quite countryside than in a city.
- At a party, will huddle with others to talk.
- Like soothing music at work.
- Are good at handling people.
- Are more open to both sides of an argument.
- May overexplain things!
- Need to be told what to do.
- Need to be listened to.
- Do not like charts and graphs.
- Use a lot of stories and metaphors
- Can be talked out of things by others.
- Use auditory words: *hear, talk, discuss, cry, buzz.*

Kinesthetic people:

- Speak very slowly and deliberately.
- Touch chest or rub chin, use gestures that draw you in.
- Look down.
- Breathe slow and deep.
- Are very casual in dress, comfort being the key.
- Need to apply feeling to thoughts ("I am not sure how I feel about this").
- Huggy, and may be moody.
- Like parties where they feel comfortable.
- Make great counselors and brilliant business people.
- Like hands-on learning.
- Can read through manipulative presentations and people.
- Do not like graphs or charts.
- May be one step ahead of others in negotiations.
- Use feeling words: *touch, grasp, handle, dig in.*

To make it even easier, nature has given us a cue to find out as to how your target is processing information. In neuro-psychogenics we call it the EYE-MOVEMENT PATTERN. This is simply automatic, unconscious eye movement that usually accompanies a particular thought process, indicating the accessing of one or more of the three primary sensory representational systems.

As a matter of fact, when people are talking, they are also thinking. And in the process of thinking and talking, they move their eyes in what are known as eye movement patterns. These movements appear to be signals of their attempts to gain access to internally stored or internally generated information in their brains. This information is encoded in the speaker's mind in one of the representational systems. When a person "goes inside," or retreats within, to retrieve a memory or to create a new thought, the person "makes pictures," and/or "talks to himself/herself," and/or "has feelings and kinesthetic sensations."

With a little bit of practice, eye-movement patterns are easily observable behavior. When you watch people talking—and, of course, simultaneously thinking—you will notice that their eyes are constantly in motion, darting back and forth, up and down, occasionally glancing at objects and people, but just as much "focused" on inner experiences. As previously stated, these movements are signals of the way they are thinking. In the descriptions that we will be discussing, "looking" would refer to the movements of a person's eyes in the direction indicated, "left" meaning toward the speaker's left, and "right" toward his/her right.

It would be helpful to keep in mind that this accessing behavior represents "looking" internally; i.e., during the moment of information retrieval, people are generally not conscious of external visual stimuli. Rather, they are concentrating on internally stored or generated images, sounds, words, and feelings. Please observe also that the words in parentheses in each category indicate the kind of information being accessed.

Internationally famous therapist Virginia Satir discovered that the eyes move as they access memories and came up with Eye-Accessing Movements.

- How you ask the question determines where your eyes will go.
- How people move their eyes tells you what part of their brain they are accessing.
- You process information internally either visually, auditorily, or kinesthetically, olfactorily, or gustatorily.

A small percentage of people are reversed. Some say if you are left-handed, this is reversed. This also varies from nation to nation. The French use more gustatory and olfactory than we do.

The easiest way to remember these is:

- If you look up, you are making pictures.
- If you look side to side, you are making sounds.
- If you look down, you are either talking to yourself or accessing a feeling.

Mind Control

Just remember: pictures, sounds, feelings, until you get used to it, then learn each side. The diagram illustrates the direction of a person's eye-accessing movements as you are facing and looking at the person.

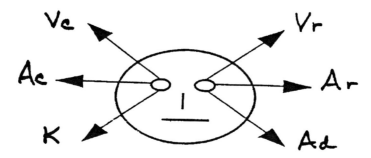

When we process information internally, the process itself can be visual, auditory, or kinesthetic. It is possible to access the meaning of a word in any one or a combination of the three primary sensory channels.

Vc	Visual Constructed:	Seeing images of things never seen before, or seeing things differently than they were seen before. Questions include: "What will you look like at ninety?"
Ac	Auditory Constructed:	Hearing sounds not heard before. Questions include: "What would your name sound like backward?" "How would a dog barking, a car horn, and children playing sound like?"
K	Kinesthetic:	Feeling emotions, tactile sensations (sense of touch), or proprioceptive feeling (feelings of muscle movement). Questions include: "Is your nose cold now?" "What does it feel like to run?"
Vr	Visual Remembered:	Seeing images of things seen before, in the same way they were seen before. Questions include: "What does your coat look like?"
Ar	Auditory Remembered:	Remembering sounds heard before. Questions include: "What's the last thing I said?" "What does your alarm clock sound like?"
Ad	Auditory Digital:	Talking to oneself. Questions include: "Say something to yourself that you often say." "Recite the Pledge of Allegiance."
V	Visual:	The blank stare is visual—either constructed or remembered.

To keep this as simple as possible while you are learning this, it is best to focus on the fact that if your target looks up, they are making a picture. If they look to the sides, they are making sounds. If they look down, they are talking to themselves or feeling something.

A good example of how you can use eye-accessing cues is in the case of a car sale. A salesman might stress different features to a customer depending on which is the customer's primary representational system in order to "step into his model of the world."

For an auditory customer, the salesman could stress the thud of the reinforced doors, the upscale stereo system, the whisper-quiet ride. To a visual customer, the salesman would stress the clean, sleek lines, the clear view of the scenery through the large tinted windows and sunroof, and ask them to picture themselves behind the wheel, etc. A kinesthetic person might respond more to the feel of the full grain leather seats, the feel of the wind in their hair, and the warm sun on their face through the sunroof as they drive along the highway.

You also have to stress that even though they have a primary system, you should try to appeal to all systems because we all use more than one. This would also take into account another person who might be involved in the decision making process, i.e., the spouse or parent accompanying the buyer, etc.

In your personal life an auditory husband might leave socks on the floor, dishes on the table, shoes in the corner, newspapers here and there. A visual wife might feel that she married a total slob who doesn't appreciate her effort to create a pleasant, tidy house. "If he loved me," she would think, "he would care that I spend all day cleaning," etc.

On the other hand, the auditory husband may come home from work and sit down to read the newspaper. Meanwhile, the wife has the food processor running making supper, the TV is on, one teenager is literally blasting the CD player, while the other is teasing a barking dog. The husband, who is auditory and trying to engage a visual task, screams, "Can't I get some peace and quiet in my own home?" Again misunderstandings can occur. It might save a trip to the divorce court if both partners realized that:

- To this wife, the visual appearance of the home or her clothes, or the lawn is important to her, but makes little impression on an auditory person.
- To this husband, the bombardment caused by of all these sounds at once would be like a visual person watching a laser show in an electrical storm!

Just understanding differences can make things run much smoother.

Further, the example of teenagers coming home late and the parents asking where they have been is one way to utilize eye-movement cues. If the teenager looks up and left, they are visually remembering and telling you where they were. If they look up and right (visual construct), it is possible they are fabricating a story that you would accept. It does not necessarily mean that they are definitely lying, but it may be that the parent ought to ask a few more questions.

Eye-Accessing Cues—A Coworker

For this exercise, ask a coworker (or business associate) to sit opposite you in a comfortable chair as you ask the following fifteen questions. Next to each question, note the eye-accessing cues you observed by writing beside each question the abbreviations in bold below:

Vc   Visual Constructed—movement up and to the person's right
Vr   Visual Remembered—movement up and to the person's left
V   Visual—movement straight ahead and eyes defocused
Ac   Auditory Constructed—movement sideways to the person's right
Ar   Auditory Remembered—movement sideways to the person's left
K   Kinesthetic—movement down and to the person's right
Ad   Auditory Digital—movement down and to the person's left

Example: How does your car's engine sound?____Ar____

1. Think of your favorite song and hum it to yourself. _____
2. Which is colder, your right or your left hand? _____
3. What would you look like if you weighted fifteen pounds less? _____
4. Who was the first person you saw yesterday? _____
5. Think about the last time someone cut you off when you were driving your car. _____
6. What does a car alarm sound like? _____
7. What does your mother's voice sound like? _____
8. When you are feeling sad, what lifts your spirits up? _____
9. How much is 125 divided by 5? _____
10. Who was the last person you spoke with before you came here? _____
11. Recite "Mary had a little lamb" silently. _____
12. What does it sound like when the television is on, the phone rings, and someone knocks on the door? _____
13. Think about the last time you felt proud of something you did. _____
14. What color are the walls in your bedroom? _____
15. Imagine what a purple dog would look like. _____

Representational Systems Overview

Seeing (Visual)

Eyes	These people look up to their right or left, or their eyes may appear unfocused.
Gestures	Their gestures are quick and angular, and include pointing.
Breathing and	High, shallow, and quick.
Speech	Fast.
Words	The words that capture their attention include: *See, look, imagine, reveal, perspective.*
Presentations	They prefer pictures, diagrams, movies.

Hearing (Auditory)

Eyes	These people look down to the left and may appear "shifty-eyed."
Gestures	Their gestures are balanced, touching one's face (i.e., rubbing the chin).
Breathing and	Midchest, rhythmic.
Speech	Speak rhythmically.
Words	The words that capture their attention include: *Hear, listen, ask, tell, clicks, in-tune.*
Presentations	They prefer lists, summaries, quotes, readings.

Feeling (Kinesthetic)

Eyes	These people look down to the right.
Gestures	Their gestures are rhythmic, touching their chest (basically true for men)—Clinton.
Breathing and	Deep, slow with pauses.
Speech	Speak slowly.
Words	The words that capture their attention include: *Feel, touch, grasp, catch on, contact.*
Presentations	Toward [Goals]: achieve, attain, gain. Away from [Problems]: avoid, relieve, out.

To be more persuasive with all groups, make the representation BIGGER, CLOSER, MORE COLORFUL, 3-D, MOVIE.

The following lists are predicates in language (verbs, adverbs, and adjectives) that have specific representational systems. A way of detecting the primary (most commonly used) representational system a person has in consciousness is by listening to the language, the sentences generated, and noticing the predicates used.

Visual	Auditory	Kinesthetic	Unspecified	Olfactory/Gust
See	Sound	Feel	Think	Smell
Picture	Hear	Relax	Decide	Fragrant
Perceive	Discuss	Grasp	Understand	Stink
Notice	Listen	Handle	Know	Reek
Look	Talk	Stress	Develop	Aroma
Show	Call on	Pressure	Prepare	Pungent
Appear	Quiet	Smooth	Activate	Sour
Clear	Inquire	Clumsy	Manage	Sweet
Pretty	Noisy	Rough	Repeat	Acrid
Colorful	Loud	Hard	Advise	Musty
Hazy	Outspoken	Grip	Indicate	Fresh
Observe	Articulate	Warm	Consider	Bland
Flash	Scream	Rush	Motivate	Stale
Focus	Pronounce	Firm	Plan	Fresh
Bright	Remark	Euphoric	Anticipate	Bitter
Scene	Resonate	Clammy	Create	Salty
Perspective	Harmony	Touch	Generate	Nutty
Imagine	Shrill	Calm	Deduce	Delicious
View	Oral	Dull	Direct	Salivate
Vista	Whimper	Burning	Achieve	Spoiled
Horizon	Mention	Stinging	Accomplish	Sniff
Make a scene	Tongue-tied	Get the drift	Initiate	Smokey
Tunnel vision	Ring a bell	Boils down to	Conclude	Bitter pill
Plainly see	Loud and clear	Hang in there	New knowledge	Fish notion
See eye-to-eye	Idle talk	Sharp as a tack	Creative option	
Mind's eye	To tell the truth	Slipped my mind	Aware of	
Bird's-eye view	Word for word	Pull some strings	Intensify	
Catch a glimpse	Rap session	Moment of panic	Incorporate	
Bright future	Unheard of	Smooth operator	Differentiate	
In light of	Call on	Get the drift	Represent	

Once you learn these, you can transpose them to their representational system. Don't be like the therapist who says, "Get in touch with your feelings," when you are a visual. Women like therapy more than men because they are more feelings oriented (kinesthetic). It is harder for men to get in touch with their feelings. A person can be thinking feelings and talking pictures. A nationally known motivational speaker and expert in the psychology of peak performance, Tony Robbins, is auditory, but represents himself visually on stage.

Always communicate in the other person's world. Use their terminology. Mirror their words, tonality, speed, etc. Using sales is all that therapy is . . . asking questions. Talk their language. Step into their model of the world.

Representational Systems Chart:

Seeing (Visual) (60 percent)

Eyes:	Look up to their left or right or may appear unfocused
Gestures:	Are quick and angular, include pointing
Breathing and speech	High, shallow, and speak quick, staccato
Words:	Visual terms: *see, look, imagine, reveal perspective*
Presentations:	Prefer pictures, diagrams, movies (eye candy) graphs, data

Hearing (Auditory) (25 percent)

Eyes:	Level left and right, down to the left (may appear shifty)
Gestures:	Rhythmic, touching one's face, (i.e., rubbing the chin), ears, mouth
Breathing and speech:	Midchest, rhythmic
Words:	Auditory terms: *hear, listen, ask, tell, click*
Presentations:	Prefer lists, summaries, quotes, readings

Feeling (Kinesthetic) (15 percent)

Eyes:	Down and to the right. Look down a lot
Gestures:	Rhythmic, touching the chest, in close
Breathing and Speech:	Deep, slow, with pauses
Words: Feeling words:	*feel, touch, grasp, catch-on, contact*
Presentations:	Toward (goals); achieve, attain, gain
	Away from (problems); avoid, relieve, out

We use all three, but there is usually a predominant. It may change by context. Someone may be visual at work and kinesthetic at home.

A kinesthetic will drive a visual crazy.

Representational systems are the most powerful stuff to influence people. How a person moves their eyes, listen to their language, step into their world.

Rapport = Really All People Prefer Others Resembling Themselves.
People like people who are like themselves. If you hear visually, feed visually back.

Unspecified:

You fill in whatever it is. If I say think, if you are visual, you will fill in with visual terms.

Training hint: If you ask, "Are there any questions?" with your hands pointing down, it will sublimate any questions. If you ask the same question with hands pointing up, you will elicit questions.

Identifying Predicates—Coworker

All of us use predicates that indicate our preferred representational systems, and your coworkers are no exception. For today, listen to the predicates used by a coworker with whom you spend a lot of time and write down each predicate you hear. When you have finished, add the number of words from each system to determine the preferred representational system.

Get the Drift—Represent

I remember being in a situation that showed how this can be lifesaving learning. As consultant to the management of a steel mill, I was trying to see how best the employees could be helped to comply with what was expected of them by the employers. While I was at it, an employee with twenty years on the job was being counseled about his drinking. He was told that he needed to stop drinking, and start attending AA meetings regularly, failing which, he faced the risk of being fired.

The counselor, who was not mirroring him—in fact, was "in his face," directly across from him—was asking him (in a very authoritative manner) how he felt about his drinking habit, and what feelings stopped him from attending AA meeting. The client responded that he did not see that he really had a problem with drinking, and, as such, he just could not see himself going to AA.

The counselor responded even before the man was finished, "How will you feel when you're fired from your job, and out on the street, after being twenty years on the job? Won't this make you feel bad?" The client responded, "I just do not see anything like this happening at all. I can't see myself out of work."

This went on for a while, before they asked for my input. I started by mirroring the client; I then asked what it would take him to "see" himself going to AA. I also had him imagine SEEING himself cleaning out his locker, as he SAW the guards waiting to escort him out the gate, for the last time. I asked him, "Can you SEE how your drinking has made the company SHOW you the door?"

The client slumped in his chair, his eyes teared up, and he asked, "Does it really look that bad? Is the future really that dark?"

I replied, "Darker than you now SEE! It is your choice to LOOK NOW at your drinking as something fine, when we all SEE a problem, a problem that will SEE you put out on the street."

"What can I do?" he asked. Now he was ready to be influenced and controlled, but he had to SEE the options and penalties.

All I did was use this technology to help this man. What the counselor did was OK; in fact it would have been brilliant if he had been a feeling person. The client was not resistant; the counselor was.

Here are some exercises to help you master decoding your target's communication style and representational systems.

Exercise 1: Celebrity Interviews

Good interviewers are able to probe people with insightful questions. Watch shows feature well-known public figures as they respond to questions. I suggest you tape a few shows, like Larry King and Oprah Winfrey, and watch them.

- Watch for eye movements, with the sound turned down. Do you notice any patterns?
- Now turn up the sound and listen to the words. Do they match the eye movements?
- Look for any down-right eye movements to tough questions.

Exercise 2: Game Shows

These shows have ordinary, real people in different situations, especially shows that make the people think and retrieve information. "Jeopardy," and "Who Wants to Be a Millionaire?" are good, to name two. Tape them, and again:

- Watch for eye-movement cues
- Listen for predicate words.

Exercise 3: Controversial Subjects

Some shows delight in the pitfalls of human conditions—Jerry Springer and the like. Watch these shows and repeat the above exercises. I also suggest you watch shows like "Meet the Press" and "Crossfire." The results are, well, eye-openers!

Here is a story submitted by a student illustrating the power of this technology and ways to practice it in real life:

> After having recently completed some of the rapport skills that Dr. Horton teaches through his beginner tape series, this is what I came up with. What makes my story all the more interesting, I believe, is the fact that:
>
> (1) I have been practicing combat martial arts for thirty years and could've used those skills instead of the rapport skills under the circumstances, and
>
> (2) I was with my four-year old boy on the day I used my rapport skills INSTEAD of my martial arts fighting skills. When I look back on it now, I realize that it was a blessing, given the fact I would never want my son to experience witnessing his father engaged in the violent act of seriously harming anyone, much less a dangerous ex-felon who might pull out a knife or a gun and try and really hurt his father or anyone else.
>
> Twenty minutes after getting on a city bus headed for downtown Los Angeles with my four-year-old son, two men got on board and sat down across from us and started sharing in hushed tones experiences about their prison lives and some of the violent crimes they had committed.
>
> I glanced over a few times, just enough to notice the telltale signs of men who've done serious time behind bars: multiple prison tattoos done with pen ink, large upper-body mass and smaller leg development, prison tans, vacant eyes with cruel expressions, and hard faces. All the signs I've learned about from the time I've spent around Orange County Sheriffs and prison guards (including a brother-in-law) who I've spoken to, personally trained, or visited at their workplaces.
>
> Having just started learning neuro-psychogenics, it hadn't yet occurred to me that I could use what I was learning in "real life" and it was not just a clinical or therapeutic situation. I was still relying on all my other "life" skills that had taken care of me up to now. In fact, I was learning NPG to promote my Pain Management/Pain Control Practice that I was struggling to get off the ground, and had spoken to Dr. Horton about ways that NFNLP could help me launch my business. The idea of using rapport skills to "connect" with someone that I would only normally "connect" with on a combat level was beyond the grasp of my mind.
>
> I quickly went through some options: Switching seats is out because the bus was overcrowded and people were in fact standing as well as sitting. There were still ten or fifteen stops to go before we got to my wife's workplace, which

put us too far away to walk (he's a sixty-pound four-year-old, which is a little heavy to carry very far). Even if we did get off the bus now, it was a bad part of town to walk through, much less wait around to catch another bus.

The fact that both of these guys were wearing army fatigue jackets and it was over ninety degrees outside didn't escape my attention, either. Then it came to me—something in the tapes that Dr. Horton referred to as "Targeting." I could start mirroring and matching their physiology. It didn't matter which one, and it didn't make sense to do both men because "targeting" doesn't work like that.

"I've got to pick just one," I told myself, so I selected the man closest to me and noticed how he was sitting. I crossed my ankles like I was a mirror reflection of him, and did the same with my arms. Whenever he moved, I waited a few seconds and then I readjusted my posture to match his. Then the bus stopped and he actually got off, leaving me with his "friend," who I immediately began pacing. I mirrored his movement at first, and then I matched it. Why mirror then match? It provided me with an opportunity to get into his particular rhythm gracefully.

After just a few minutes, I began noticing the rise-and-fall rhythm of his shoulders and thought I would make an effort to mirror his breathing patterns. He also had a habit of folding his arms across his chest, which made it easier to calibrate his breathing. Before I knew it, I was pacing his physiology INCLUDING his breathing. He even looked at his watch a few times, after which I looked at mine.

Ten, maybe fifteen minutes went by, and the bus slowly emptied out as my son and I approached our destination. People got away from this "mean-looking" guy as quickly as possible. I sat there, using my rapport skills, confident, very confident, that I was actually connecting with this ex-con on an unconscious level. And before I thought of testing to see if we were in rapport by leading him, guess what!

Three stops before I was to get off the bus with my son—are you ready?— he leans forward and actually manages what I'll consider a smile—showing four upper teeth and all! And, like we're cell mates, he asks me, "Hey, man, does this bus go all the way into Venice?"

"I'm pretty sure it does" was my response, but I made sure to answer after a brief hesitation, because I wanted him to think I was really reading a newspaper I had been pretending to read to mirror the magazine he was reading.

"Thanks, man." He then glanced at my son, winked at him, and then went back to his magazine. The wink unnerved me a little, I have to admit, but better a wink than an icy stare, right?

For those readers who don't understand hard-core violent prison types—when you're in their presence (especially if there are two or more of them!)—the response I got from this man speaks volumes about the rapport I achieved with him in the short period of time I paced him. You would have had to be there to get the full effect, and reading my words, short of a VAKOG novella, doesn't do the experience justice. All I can say is, I was initially ready to go into combat mode based on my instincts, and I ended up using rapport techniques! You be the judge.

Did I use combat rapport skills? Absolutely! Just like the combat martial arts I practice. Only it's taken me thirty years to achieve the skill level I'm at today with my mind and body as it pertains to martial arts. Whereas it literally took me as long as it takes to watch the "rapport" part of the tapes to learn the rapport skills that I used on the bus that day. I had to write this to let everyone know that I am just a beginner, and all I did was "paint by numbers" with what Dr. Horton taught.

CHAPTER 5

The Third Key
Effective Listening and Putting It Together

Now that you understand the basics of both rapport and communication styles, it is time to put them together. When you mirror and match someone physically, you also want to match their language and eye movements. This helps further deepen your level of rapport. When you do this consciously, you make your target feel comfortable, almost as though the two of you have known each other for years.

IMPORTANT NOTE: Although being liked can be a by-product of rapport, it is important to remember that rapport is much more than simply being liked. To become the kind of master of mental science, one who easily and fully establishes rapport with others, you must become an exquisite partner in the communication dance. To seek rapport with others is to invite them to dance, and then influence them in a manner that is persuasive, decisive, and, at the same time, smooth and elegant throughout the interaction, even as you reach a mutually desirable outcome.

You might find it useful to think of rapport as how responsive the other person is to you and your positive intentions. You create rapport by being responsive to the other person through pacing and mirroring that person's verbal and nonverbal behavior. The most basic rule of human nature is that people are primarily interested in talking about themselves and what they want. They are not really interested in what you think or want.

To master rapport, you must accept the fact that you have to meet and accept people for who they are, not what you think they are or should be. A person's thoughts are usually governed by self-interest. Rapport skills give you the upper hand in skillfully getting your way, though in a very subtle manner. When you let people talk about themselves or something they are passionate about, they will be deeply interested and will ultimately think you're a genius and great conversationalist! To do this, you must learn to give up words like *I*, *me*, and *mine*. These must become the smallest part of your vocabulary. So consciously pick your words because your target is the important thing to focus on.

If you give up the satisfaction you get from talking about yourself and the pleasure you get from using *I, me, mine,* your personal power will be exponentially increased. This will take some practice. It is normal to talk about yourself, but as you learn this technique, you will master this skill easily.

Also, you must understand one universal trait of all human beings, a trait so strong it makes us do a lot of the things that we do, good and bad. This is the DESIRE TO FEEL IMPORTANT and BE RECOGNIZED.

The more important you make people feel, the more they will respond to you. Pretend everyone you meet has a huge, bright sign around their neck that says: "MAKE ME FEEL IMPORTANT!"

The power of mirroring and matching allows you this special opportunity. Rapport skills will enhance your life and make you a great communicator. People will want to do what you want them to. When people tell me they have problems with rapport techniques, the biggest problem is they start with the techniques and then veer into talking about themselves. This kills rapport.

Exercises to Make People Glad They Talked to You!

Imagine someone of great importance, like the president, a famous movie star, or perhaps your idol, just came through the door. What would your initial reaction be? Most people do a quick intake of air, a slight gasp. This quick intake of air is how we show HONOR and RESPECT at the subconscious level.

When you first meet someone, and every time after that, if you take a moment to acknowledge that person in this way, then act pleased to meet them. This will make them feel noticed, respected, and important (Bill Clinton was a master at this skill, and people wanted to be around him. So was Ronald Reagan).

Here are some exercises to ingrain these skills in your subconscious:

1. Exercise 1: Go to a coffee shop or restaurant and start a conversation with someone who is unlike you—the last person you would normally talk to. Use your rapport skills and focus on them; get them to talk to you (remember to talk little or none about you).
2. Exercise 2: At work, target someone from a distance, make contact after a few minutes, and again mirror and match at all levels and see where this takes you.
3. Exercise 3: Go to a department store, look for an obscure item, and ask an attendant for help. As you are being assisted, turn on your rapport skills. Ask them how they came to work there, where they are going next, etc.

4. Exercise 4: Get one of the goals you had in mind in buying this book. Now go and use your skills in this area.

Here are some tips to help you listen as you work at building rapport skills.

The first step in developing good listening skills is to become aware of why listening is important in your professional life and personal relationships. The second step is to practice using active listening skills.

I had the opportunity to be the only non-law-enforcement person to attend the Federal Bureau of Investigations Crisis (Hostage) Negotiation course at the FBI Academy. The heart of this course is the concept of active listening. People have a tendency to think of listening as a passive activity, when the opposite is true.

What's interesting to those of us studying this field is these are the people who deal daily with getting others to do what they want. They have found the key lies in truly listening to the target, and getting them to reveal the information they need. The natural drawback in most people is they have the desire to talk too much. We are trained in most fields to gather information, then make a decision and move on. What happens is we do not spend enough time letting the other person tell their story. Hostage negotiators have found it more effective to talk the person out. And this calls for tremendous patience in listening in order to formulate a plan for the safe release of the hostages.

Let's take a cue from these experts and make this a part of our skills!

Guidelines for Good Listening:

*   Remember the rule to make them "feel important"!
*   Never interrupt when the other person is speaking. Allow the speaker to complete his/her thought.
*   Eliminate distractions.
*   Maintain eye contact with the speaker, without giving the impression of "staring."
*   Show interest by pulling your chair closer and leaning forward.
*   Keep your posture aligned with that of your target—mirror and match.
*   Give verbal and nonverbal responses to what the speaker is saying.

Listening is a skill that improves with practice, but common obstacles to good listening can impede your progress. It seems obvious that having the television set on during a conversation would be a distraction and an obstacle to good listening. But our own attitudes and personality traits can become an obstacle to listening. We must take an honest look at ourselves, and how we deal with the world, to remove these obstacles. People who tend to be mistrustful, or take a combative stance toward others, may find it difficult to engage in healthy and open listening. The same is true for people who get gratification from pleasing others besides other forms of dependency—it becomes difficult to truly hear what people are trying to say when a person hears only what he needs to hear.

Common Obstacles to Listening

- *Being Judgmental:* You listen only to gain support for the negative images you already have.
- *Rehearsing:* You actively create your argument against the speaker's point of view as it is being presented.
- *Mind Reading:* You may disregard what the speaker is saying and try to surmise what they really mean.
- *Advising:* Giving advice, instead of just listening, to make yourself feel needed. (Or it may be a way of distancing yourself from the speaker's true feelings.)
- *Pleasing:* You are so concerned about being nice and placating that you will not hesitate to interrupt to agree just in order to maintain peace. But it prevents you from hearing what the speaker needs to say.
- *Filtering:* You will hear some things the speaker says, but not everything.
- *Deflecting:* You redirect by changing the subject or telling a joke when the topic is uncomfortable for you.

Listening is more than passively being quiet while the speaker talks. It is half of an active collaborative method of communication. The first level is attentive listening. For this type of listening, we convey that we are genuinely interested in the speaker's point of view and what he has to say. The second level of listening is active listening. This type of listening assumes that communication is a two-way process, which involves giving feedback or reflecting the speaker.

Active listening requires the listener to paraphrase, clarify, and give feedback.

Paraphrasing is a vital component of active listening. By restating in your own words what the speaker said, you are able to correct misconceptions as they occur and overcome the obstacles to listening. The speaker feels he has been heard and is understood.

Clarifying provides more depth to the listening process than exclusively using paraphrasing. The purpose of clarifying is to ask questions about what the speaker is saying in an empathic and helpful way. Clarifying tells the speaker you are really interested and want to know more about specific areas.

Giving feedback involves providing your own thoughts on what the speaker has said, while avoiding the obstacles to good listening. This gives the speaker another opportunity to see you understand him. When we listen well to the speaker, we not only show that person care and respect, but we also show we are open to the world around us.

Listening to Children

Childhood is when people develop a level of self-esteem that may be with them throughout their lifetime. Indeed, a child who has been listened to is much more likely to develop a positive self-image than one who has not been heard. Listening to children makes them feel they matter! Children need to be heard too.

Use the following listening techniques to address the special needs of children:

1. Pay special attention as the child talks to you. Maintain good eye contact and eliminate distractions—all distractions. Children can tell by an adult's reply whether or not they have your full attention.
2. Listen with due patience. Listen as if you have plenty of time. A child's vocabulary is often limited. Frequently repetitive in their use of words, it may take them longer to express their ideas.
3. Children sometimes need encouragement to talk. Children are generally inexperienced in the art of conversation, so the adult will have to ask some questions. A child is more willing to open up when he feels that an adult is really attentive.
4. Listen to the child's nonverbal messages. Children communicate not only through words, but also through their body language, facial expressions, tone of voice, energy levels, and changes in behavior. Pay attention to the cues and respond in the way that is best for the child.
5. Pay attention to the child's mood, and be sure the time and setting is right for the child to talk. Sometimes a child just wants to play or be left alone. Being playful with a child who wishes to play may also encourage them to open up.

Another thing that will help you sharpen your listening and communication skills at this level is to eliminate negatives from your vocabulary. One of the most important principles of good communication is that success is measured according to whether what you do works.

What Does "Don't" Mean?

There is a stupid question if there ever was one! Everyone knows *don't* means **do not**. So is this a trick question or what? Let's find out.

Don't think of Santa Claus! I have the feeling you now have an internal picture of the little man with a long white beard in the famous red suit. Or you heard a voice, internally, saying, "Merry Christmas! Ho! Ho! Ho!" and it was your idea of the voice of Santa. You may have had a feeling of the fat man himself, or a smell or taste of Christmas perhaps.

Don't think of how old you are.

You thought of your age or your birth date, right?

The mind only works in positives. For the mind to understand and process what you do not want to happen, the brain must first think about doing the action before it can even consider not doing it. For instance, if I say to my client, "Don't think of my competitor's product for this job," for his brain to make sense of that statement, there must first be a representation of my competitor's product (and maybe how it would fit this job!). If you tell a child, "Don't play in the street," they must first have an internal representation of playing in the street. Remember this when you tell your assistant, "Don't be late for this next meeting."

The classic statement we hear all the time is "Don't worry." In order to refrain from worrying and make sense of the directive ("Don't worry"), the listener must first have an idea of worrying. Have you ever heard someone say to a salesperson, "Don't worry about your sales slump." It would be much better to say, "Be assured, you'll be fine." or "Relax, and focus on the positives. We all go through this."

The focus must always be on the desired outcome, or purpose, of the communication, and the extent to which outcome is achieved. To transfer understanding from yourself to another person, you need to make sure what you are saying nonverbally supports what you are saying verbally. Your state of mind and how you feel will affect the information you are trying to convey.

To illustrate, here's an interesting exercise.

Negative/Positive Outcomes Exercise

To ascertain the power of negative and positive outcomes, do the following exercise. Find a quiet place where you can concentrate without any distractions. This includes turning off any television or radio that may be playing in the background.

Words Associated with Negative Outcome

Think about an event you do not want to happen or a situation you would find unpleasant or distasteful. This could be anything: your career, a personal relationship, a project you are working on—whatever. Concentrate on the event for a few minutes. Put yourself totally in the situation. Hear the sounds, picture the event, experience the feelings, etc. Notice the words that come to mind when you think of the negative outcome of that experience.

Words Associated with Positive Outcome

Now think of the same situation, but this time, in a positive sense. Mentally, experience fully all of the positive aspects. Put yourself totally in the situation, hear the sounds, picture the event, experience the feelings, etc. Think about how great you will feel when you achieve what you want. Notice the words that come to mind when you think of the positive outcome of that experience.

ı of the two above scenarios did you prefer? Probably the one with the positive
. The difference between the two events is not just in the mind. If someone had
been watching you, they would have noticed a difference in your facial expression, your
breathing, and your body posture. Physiologically, you become what you think about.
The difference between success and failure is how you envision your outcome.

Concentrating on what you don't want to happen, sometimes known as worrying, can
have a negative impact on more than just your physical body. It has to do with how your
brain processes outcomes and desires. Your brain ignores negatives. You may say to yourself,
"I don't want to be late for the meeting," but what your brain registers is LATE. The way to
"trick" your brain, if you will, is to tell yourself, "I want to get to the meeting ten minutes
early." Your brain hears "early," and that is what it records as your desired outcome.

It may be difficult at first to eliminate negatives from your thoughts and speech,
but with a little practice it can be done. You will be amazed by the results. For practice,
complete the next exercise. Then we will return to the best way to create the outcomes
that will give you the results you want.

Eliminating Negative Suggestions Exercise

Most of us use the "don't" word on a regular basis. We say things like, "Don't forget
to pick up bread and milk on the way home." What the brain hears is, "Forget to pick
up bread and milk." I can assure you that is exactly what happened. You forgot the
bread and milk.

For this exercise, keep track of how many times you hear the word "don't" used
around you. If possible, write the sentences down. Advertisements can be a good source
of negative suggestions. Beneath each sentence, write a more positive way to express
the desired outcome. (Note: You may want to carry around a pocket notebook so you
can jot the sentences down as you hear them.)

Negative Suggestion: Don't forget to call the client about tomorrow's meeting.
Positive Suggestion: Let the client know we'll be meeting tomorrow.

Negative Suggestion: Don't put that file away; I'm not done looking it over.
Positive Suggestion: Keep that file out until I'm done looking it over.

REMEMBER TO TELL PEOPLE WHAT YOU WANT THEM TO DO!

You can also decide to tell them the opposite. Such as in a personal setting, "Don't
think about how much fun it would be to go out with me tonight." In a business arena,
"Yes, that other model is a nice car. Don't think about how it was recalled last year for
safety reasons. I'm sure it's fine now."

If you practice these skills, you will be amazed how you will be able to get people to
follow you in ways you never thought possible. Use these skills with respect and honor.

Thought Awareness, Rational Thinking, and Positive Thinking

These three related tools are useful in combating negative thinking. Negative thoughts occur when you put yourself down, criticize yourself for errors, doubt your abilities, expect failure, etc. Negative thinking is the negative side of suggestion—just as making positive statements to yourself helps you to build confidence, improve performance, and improve your mental skills, negative thinking damages these things.

Thought Awareness

Thought awareness is the process by which you observe your thoughts for a time, perhaps during a performance or a training session, and are aware of the thoughts going through your head. It is best not to suppress any thoughts—just let them run their course while you observe them.

Watch for negative thoughts while you observe your "stream of consciousness." Normally these will appear and disappear being barely noticed. Normally you may not even notice them. Examples of common negative thoughts are:

- worries about performance
- a preoccupation with the symptoms of stress
- dwelling on consequences of poor performance
- self-criticism
- feelings of inadequacy

Make a note, whether mental or physical, of the thought, and then let the stream of consciousness run on. Thought awareness is the first step in the process of eliminating negative thoughts—you cannot counter thoughts you do not know you think.

Rational Thinking

Once you are aware of your negative thoughts, write them down and review them rationally. See whether the thoughts have any basis in reality. Often you will find that when you challenge negative thoughts, they disappear as you see that they are obviously wrong. Often they persist only because they escape notice.

Positive Thinking and Affirmation

You may find it useful to counter negative thoughts with positive affirmations. You can use affirmations to build confidence and change negative behavior patterns into positive ones. You can base affirmations on clear, rational assessments of fact, and use them to undo the damage that negative thinking may have done to your self-confidence.

Examples of affirmations are:

> - I can achieve my goals.
> - I am completely myself and people will like me for myself.
> - I am completely in control of my life.
> - I learn from my mistakes. They increase the basis of experience on which I can draw.
> - I am a good valued person in my own right.

Traditionally people have advocated positive thinking almost recklessly, as a solution to everything. It should, however, be used with common sense: no amount of positive thinking will make everyone who applies it an Olympic champion marathon runner (although an Olympic marathon runner is unlikely to have reached this level without being pretty good at positive thinking). Firstly decide rationally what goals you can realistically attain with hard work, and then use positive thinking to reinforce these.

More Information to include from the work of Dr. Totko and Dr. Olgilive, considered by many the leaders in sports psychology.

All of the questions are to be answered either True or False

1. Under high levels of stress, athletes typically have a broad attention span. **T or F**
2. The clammy feeling we often get when stressed is caused by our body's natural defense against bleeding to death. **T or F**
3. Elite level performers have fewer nervous reactions to stress than do nonelite level performers. **T or F**
4. High levels of stress make it more difficult to think clearly. **T or F**
5. Getting sick to your stomach and throwing up when nervous is your body's way of telling you that you are overstressed. **T or F**
6. Caffeine exaggerates the physical and mental effects of stress. **T or F**
7. The body's stress response, which is commonly referred to as the fight-or-flight response, allows us to do superhuman feats. **T or F**
8. The only time stress is good is when there is no stress. **T or F**
9. Sighing as you exhale is more relaxing than not sighing. **T or F**
10. Under stress, athletes often revert back to their most well learned behaviors. **T or F**

Answer Key

1. **False.** Under high levels of stress, athletes tend to have a narrow attention span, often referred to as tunnel vision. Attention may also focus on the athlete's internal thought process which can lead to "choking" under pressure.

2. **True.** One of the physical responses of the body to stress is to divert blood away from the small vessels near the skin. This provides a defense against bleeding to death from wounds, but gives the skin a cold, clammy feeling.

3. **False.** Elite-level performers have just as many nervous reactions to stress as any other type of performer. However, elite athletes often interpret these reactions as being more positive and beneficial than do other athletes.

4. **True.** Clear thinking is more difficult in pressure situations. This is why coaches and athletes must constantly practice what they are going to do and how they are going to respond in pressure-packed situations.

5. **False.** So that more blood is available to the large muscles of the body in preparation for strenuous physical activity such as fighting or running away, the digestive system shuts down. During this shutdown, the acid in your stomach makes you feel nauseated which sometimes results in throwing up. This is a normal reaction to stress.

6. **True.** Caffeine tends to exaggerate the physical and mental effects of stress. Knowing this, coaches and athletes should avoid caffeine products before entering potentially stressful situations.

7. **True.** Under stress, the body produces adrenalin, which provides a powerful, quick burst of energy sometimes resulting in superhuman feats.

8. **False.** There are a number of stresses which are good. For example, being elevated to the starting team brings additional stress which most athletes would enjoy. Another example of positive stress is physical and mental training. All athletes are under stress when, during training, they push themselves to the edge so that their body will adapt to the demand and get stronger.

9. **True.** For some reason, letting out an audible sigh as you exhale is very relaxing. There are a number of additional relaxation techniques which involve breathing exercises.

10. **True.** In stressful situations, athletes often revert back to behaviors they are familiar and comfortable with. This is one of the reasons why athletes should try to learn and perfect new skills and techniques in the off-season.

In conclusion, your reaction to stress will affect every cell in your body. Regardless if the reasons are real or imaginary, your reactions are similar. We each have a biological alarm clock that goes off automatically, whether we want it to or not. This reaction is valuable if you are about to be hit by a car but it has disadvantages if you are trying to settle down and concentrate on your game. By knowing what the reactions are, athletes can learn to interpret these responses as being normal and perhaps even beneficial to their performance.

References:

Tutko, T., and Tosi, U. (1976). *Sports psyching: Playing your best game all of the time.* New York: Putnam Publishing.

Olgilvie, B. Pro-mind.com

CHAPTER 6

Strategies

Have you ever seen people at a restaurant trying to decide what they will order? They may look up, pause, look down, lick their lips, touch their stomach, then order something; or they may repeat the options to themselves. (In their heads, or sometimes out loud, "a quarter-pound cheeseburger, hmm.") They may even ask someone else, "What's good?" (Hope your tastes are similar!) Whatever they do, they are running some type of strategy, and most, if not all, of it is preconscious. We are not aware of how we do it. We just do it.

Psychology tells us that it is a learned behavior, which it is. But once learned, it is put out of our conscious awareness. Even a Pavlovian response can be considered a learned strategy. Think about the classical Pavlov training. A dog is repeatedly presented with food, and a bell is rung. Eventually, the bell alone will elicit a saliva response in the dog. Somewhere in that dog's brain it is learning: Bell = food = eat, or, Food = bell = eat. So it is with humans. We learn a strategy and then we use it over and over, until we replace or change it.

The problems begin to take place when our strategies are no longer working, or when we use an inappropriate strategy. You see this when someone uses a strategy that works in business (profit and loss) in their personal relationships. They bail at the first hint of effort.

To make this easy to learn, think about what you ate the last time you went to a restaurant. How did you decide what to have? Did you look at the menu (visual), then mentally taste the food (gustatory or kinesthetic)? Possibly you said something to yourself (auditory), when you found something you wished to order. Then you exited the program. An aside: one reason it is difficult for some people to order food when they are really hungry is that they get stuck in the program; they keep playing options ("That sounds good, that looks good, I always liked that . . ." etc).

You have a strategy for EVERYTHING you do, and a lot of those strategies overlap. You may use the same style of strategy in different contexts. This may or may not be problematic. I worked with a man who used his business strategy (which made him rich) to find a wife. He found his prospect (business venture), did his research (dating), found he wanted to acquire the property, and was willing to pay the asking rate (marriage). So they got married. He then took a hands-off approach, paid the price, and bought the house and cars—now he was basically ignoring his wife, unless there was a problem (the way he would run a business). What he actually needed was a romantic strategy.

The good part is you can change, install, or remove a strategy. This is one of the things we do with hypnotic suggestions.

People have their own strategy for everything they do. They will use these strategies when they communicate. These strategies are the primary (or lead), secondary, and tertiary representational systems of the person. For example, a person can use a VISUAL, AUDITORY or KINESTHETIC strategy for buying a car. SEE a car you really like; HEAR good things about the car; drive the car and it FEELS good; buy the car, then rationalize the costs.

There are a lot of nuances to strategies. There are internal and external cues, as well as what are known as META programs. These are strategies you use in every situation, and you use them to develop other strategies. We will go into those later. But I want to show you how you can use this information today in your work.

First, when a new client calls, ask them what they need to help them make a decision about your services. Then listen to what and how they say it. Do they need to hear from others that hypnosis worked for them? Do they want to see something in print about you? Do they want to feel comfortable with you? Repeat back what they say, and then give them what they want, or tell them you will supply them with what they need when they come in. Once they agree to come in, the odds are they will become a client.

Second, when you have a weight-loss client, ask them as to how they know when it is time to eat. Do they see others eating? At dinnertime, do they feel they must eat? When they see food, is their first response to eat? Or do they feel they must eat when they feel good? Or feel the need to eat when they feel bad? You will find a lot of our clients do not use HUNGER as a cue to eat. A naturally thin person will almost always use HUNGER as the key cue of when to eat. They will not eat if they are not hungry, so they are seldom overweight.

Third, try installing the following eating strategy for a few of your clients. You can do this by having them mentally rehearse the program while in a trance.

The next time you're presented with a stimulus for food (by seeing others eating, or when it's dinnertime), check your stomach to see if you are hungry. If not, exit, saying to yourself, "You are not hungry. There is no reason to eat." If you are hungry, ask yourself, "What would taste good and help me to achieve my other goals (weight loss, getting in shape, etc.)?" Imagine tasting the food and thinking, "How will this feel, later?" If the reply is negative, repeat the selection process until you find a healthy choice. Reinforce this with direct hypnosis, and you will be amazed how this will add to (or subtract from) your clients' results.

The following example is how I used strategies in a clinical setting. I had a client on whom I had been using hypnosis as a form of therapy. This client had tried hypnosis in the past for weight loss with limited success. Now she was stuck. She would do very well at work and through the main part of the day. She would have a small piece of fruit in the morning and a light lunch if she was hungry, or she would walk and not stop after work for a snack. She was making notable progress. She would, however, start eating at night and would overeat. Since she had used hypnosis with some success, I thought we would see what her strategy was for night eating.

She relaxed and I asked her what happened when she got home. At first she just said, "It seems like I walk in and start eating."

"So you have a refrigerator by your door?" I asked. "Tell me what happens as you walk inside your door."

"Well, I open the door and I see an empty apartment." She was divorced, and her youngest was in college.

"Then what?" I prompted.

"I hear a voice that says a woman is not supposed to be alone."

"Whose voice?" I asked.

"My mother's."

"Then what happens?" I asked.

"I feel bad, like a little girl, a bad little girl," she replied softly.

"Then what?" I probed.

"I hear another voice and it says, 'EAT SOMETHING. YOU'LL FEEL BETTER' (Her mother again).

"Then what do you do?" I prompted.

"I eat something, and I feel a little better. Then I feel guilty because I'm supposed to be trying to lose weight."

"Anything else?" I ask.

"I hear that voice again: 'EAT SOMETHING! YOU'LL FEEL BETTER!'" And off she'd go on a binge again!

The technique I decided to use was to bypass the whole mess. When she opened the door she would say to herself it was so nice to choose to live alone. She would also make plans to do things she had put off for years: dance class, movies, etc. We also did some reparenting about the intent of what her mother meant. This client did quite well.

I urge you to track your internal processes when you are making decisions so you can learn about strategies firsthand. This is an advanced NLP process, but once you are comfortable with the idea, it will get easier, and it can be a very useful tool to learn more about how people think. Remember the *why* is not very useful. In the above example, we could have spent a lot of time on why. Why had her mother behaved so? But if we change the behavior first, we remove the emotional charge. Then we can change the program.

Motivational Metaprograms:

How people process information that influences their behavior.

Metaprogram Type	Choice Points
1. Decision Making	Self
	Others
	Data/Information
2. Decision Rules	Values
	Beliefs
3. Matching	Direct Match
	Direct Mismatch
	Mismatch with Exceptions
4. Information Requirements	General
	Specific/Systematic
5. Information Order	Sequential
	Random
6. Time References (Can be combined with Matching and Approach/Avoidance)	Past
	Present
	Future
7. Time Relationships	Patient
	Impatient
8. Approach/Avoidance Move Toward/Move Away From	Pleasure/Goal
	Pain/Problem/Conflict
9. Financial	Cost
	Convenience
10. Quality	Price
	Value
11. Frame of Reference (Locus of Control)	Internal
	External
12. Interactive	Interpersonal (Others)
	Intrapersonal (Self)
13. Priority	High
	Low
14. Work	Independent
	Cooperative (Group)
15. Security/Stability	Necessity
	Possibility/Risk

16. Focus	Global/Broad/General
	Narrow/Specific
17. Rationality	Logic/Thought/Objectivity
	Emotions/Feelings/Impulse
18. Buying Criteria	What
	When
	Who
	How
	Why
19. Attitude	Positive
	Negative
20. Source of Motivation	Intrinsic (Self Rewards)
	Extrinsic (External Rewards)

Submodality Distinctions

Modality	Submodality	Questions
Visual	Color/Black-and-White	• Is it in color or black-and-white? • Is it full-color spectrum? • Are the colors vivid or washed out?
	Brightness	In that context, is it brighter or darker than normal?
	Contrast	Is it high contrast (vivid) or washed out?
	Focus	Is the image sharp in focus, or is it fuzzy?
	Texture	Is the image smooth or rough textured?
	Detail	• Are there foreground and background details? • Do you see the details as part of a whole, or do you have to shift focus to see them?
	Size	How big is the picture? (ask for specific size)
	Distance	How far away is the image? (specific distance)
	Shape	What shape is the picture: square, rectangular, round?
	Border	• Is there a border around it, or do the edges fuzz out? • Does the border have a color? • How thick is the border?
	Location	• Where is the image located in space? • Show me with both hands where you see the images(s).

	Movement	• Is it a movie or a still picture? • How rapid is the movement: faster or slower than normal? • Is the image stable? • What direction does it move in? • How fast is it moving?
	Orientation	Is the picture tilted?
	Association / Dissociation	Do you see yourself, or do you see the event as if you were there?
	Perspective	• From what perspective do you see it? • (If dissociated) Do you see yourself from the right or left, back or front?
	Proportion	Are there people and things in the image in proportion to one another and to you, or are some of them larger or smaller than life?
	Dimension	• Is it flat, or is it three-dimensional? • Does the picture wrap around you?
	Singular / Plural	• Is there one image or more than one? • Do you see them one after the other or at the same time?
Auditory	*Location*	• Do you hear it from the inside or from the outside? • Where does the sound (voice) originate?
	Pitch	• Is it high-pitched or low-pitched? • Is the pitch higher or lower than normal?
	Tonality	What is the tonality: nasal, full and rich, think, grating?
	Melody	Is it a monotone, or is there a melodic range?
	Inflection	Which parts are accentuated?
	Volume	How loud is it?
	Tempo	Is it fast or slow?
	Rhythm	Does it have a beat or a cadence?
	Duration	Is it continuous or intermittent?
	Mono / Stereo	Do you hear it on one side, both sides, or is the sound all around you?
Kinesthetic	Intensity	How strong is the sensation?
	Quality	How would you describe the body sensations: tingling, warm, cold, relaxed, tense, knotted, diffused?

	Location	Where do you feel it in your body?
	Movement	• Is there movement in the sensation? • Is the movement continuous, or does it come in waves?
	Direction	• Where does the sensation start? • How does it get from the place of origin to the place where you are most aware of it?
	Speed	Is it a slow, steady progression, or does it move in a rush?
	Duration	Is it continuous or intermittent?

I would like to tell you a little something about a guy named Ron. When Ron was getting ready to start his martial arts school, he knew it was a competitive business. Most karate schools fail in the first year, and very few schools make enough for the owner to not have to take up another full-time job. Ron decided the first thing he needed to do was find schools where the owner was making a good living at teaching martial arts. (One effective strategy is to find someone who has done what you want to do, and do what they did. This is called *modeling*.) So he took some time and visited a few successful schools.

The first thing he noticed was the schools signing up a lot of students seemed to fit their selling style to the client's needs and wants, rather than to the head teacher's agenda.

An example: a young man comes in interested in classes. The first thing the successful people did was to find out WHY the person was looking into learning martial arts. If he was looking for self-esteem, they would discuss how the martial arts would build that. If it was physical fitness, they would talk up the workout part and the flexibility you acquire. Self-defense? Well, the teacher would talk up how you would be able to defend yourself. Self-discipline—that's what martial arts are all about!

Ron also noticed if a parent brought in a child, the teacher would do the same thing to both the parent and the child. He would then talk up the points the parent wanted and the points the child wanted.

Ron took special note how the teacher would ask each prospective client how they would know when they found the school that fit their needs the best. The teacher would listen, taking note of what they said—such as the prospect who said, "Well, I will see that the students have respect, that they have done well in competition, and probably I would want a free class or two." After some more general talk about the martial arts, the teacher showed the prospective student some of the trophies they had won at recent events. He then asked a current student what this school's attitude was, and the student named several; and when he said RESPECT, the teacher stopped him and said to the prospective client, "Respect is important here—very important indeed!" He then invited the student for a trial workout.

Ron was amazed. He knew this technology, and had just watched this teacher get into rapport, match the client, get his strategy, find out which of the core desires was most important (accomplishment, belonging, and value), and then feed it back to the client. The client signed up before he left that evening.

Ron then watched as the teacher did the same to a mother and son. The mother wanted self-discipline and physical fitness; the son wanted to learn how to defend himself. The teacher repeated back the benefits each wanted and how his martial arts school was the answer. The teacher then asked the mother how she would ascertain whether she had found the right place for her son. She stated the place had to be clean, well run, and friendly. Of course, the teacher pointed out how clean this operation was and emphasized that the classes start on time and finish on time, and how it was like a big family—yes, students' family members are welcome to watch classes. The mother signed her son up then and there!

Ron saw what he needed. But just to be sure, he went to a couple of other schools and got a tour. Here the teacher proceeded to tell him why his school was the best, and he never once asked any questions. The same thing happened at a couple of other smaller schools. Ron saw why the first school he contacted was growing by leaps and bounds, while in the case of these others, the teachers had to hold second jobs just to make a living.

The above was an example of strategies, how people put together how they think (the visual, auditory, kinesthetic) with the sixteen basic desires to come up with an unconscious process of deciding how to decide.

Martial Arts Story

A guy went to Japan to study with the martial arts experts. There were two masters. He asked all kinds of questions until one of the instructors suggested they have tea.

He started pouring tea into a teacup and kept pouring until the cup overflowed. The student finally stopped the instructor and asked why he was letting the tea pour out of the cup.

The analogy is that the student's mind was so full that the instructors could not put any more information in, and until the student emptied his mind, he could not learn.

The comparison to martial arts is that NLP techniques are a powerful, potentially manipulative technology that could be used for good or bad just like martial arts.

Milton Erickson

Called the father of clinical hypnotherapy, Milton Erickson was a good storyteller using the metaphors and analogies.

He liked to use tasks as learning experiences. One incident was asking students to climb a mountain to get them out of the office. They would come back with wonderful metaphors about the struggles of life, etc.

Give everyone a string. The string is a metaphor. Put it on your wrist. Develop your own metaphor. No one can pull your string anymore. Take the string off at the end of the class upon graduation.

Leave the string on for the full time you are in the class. Then tell the class what your metaphor for the string means.

You can now begin focusing on how your brain makes sense of the world.

CHAPTER 7

Anchoring

Anchor Your Way to Success

"It doesn't count if you don't get caught," an NFL coach once said regarding some bad calls that went his way during a game.

In the 1996 presidential election, we got to watch Bill Clinton pull off some of the best examples of anchoring the world has ever seen, and very few people even noticed. At one point in the debates, President Clinton walked center stage and listed several facts about the state of the union at that time.

- The economy is booming.
- More jobs have been created in the last four years than in the previous twelve.
- Unemployment was at an all-time low.
- We were at peace.

After he listed all these wonderful things, he made the comment, "I can't take all the credit for all the good things that have happened these last few years."

Great comment, but as he said, "all the good things that have happened," he touched his tie. Each time he said a great positive thing about the country, he touched his tie or face. He was anchoring all those positives to himself.

But that was not enough; he went on to say, "We still have problems in this country, people are being left behind." As he said this, he made a gesture with his hand toward Bob Dole.

If you were watching the debates, you were using your conscious mind to track the information while your subconscious was wide open for this type of salesmanship. This could explain the great public ambivalence toward Bill Clinton. In our subconscious minds he is anchored to good things. (Not just to pick on Clinton, Ronald Regan also did this brilliantly, anchoring positive things to himself.)

Often in the process of communicating, the achieved level of rapport can diminish in the middle of the transaction! The secret technique many successful people use to quickly reestablish the initial rapport is called anchoring. Below are the basics of anchoring:

1) It does not take a long period of time to establish an anchor. Repeated motivations and conditioning will reinforce an anchor.

2) Reinforcement and direct rewards are not required for an anchor's association.

3) Internal responses and experiences are significant. Although internal reactions are not measurable, they are a definitive response.

4) Anchors are "set" and "fired." The more profound the experience when the catalyst is set, the stronger the retaliatory response.

5) Timing is crucial while establishing an anchor. It is necessary that the correct trigger sets off the desired response. The strength of the response will guide the client's mind in the necessary and desired path.

6) The more original the motivation, the easier reestablishing the desired rapport. The repercussions of mixed responses due to general stimuli could often be detrimental to the client as well as the relationship as a whole. By establishing unique stimuli, it allows for little margin of error and ease of reassessing the desired state.

7) Anchors can be established in the visual, auditory, and kinesthetic representational systems.

Anchors can be set and fired both consciously and unconsciously. People regularly create anchors in everyday experiences. They may watch a news show about an incident or situation they feel strongly about (negative or positive). From that point on, any time a word comes up that brings forth the memory of that news show, it will elicit a certain response. In effect, an anchor has been "set" and "fired off."

One way to think of it is the old bell curve. As you enter into any "state" (emotional experience), it will usually start slow and build to a peak, then diminish. If something happens, a unique stimulus is applied. As you are hitting the peak of the feeling, that stimulus will cause you to enter into that same "state" or emotion.

Think of the power of this in your daily transactions. If you could anchor the people you deal with into positive emotional states, would that not help you in the relationship?

Here are some examples of anchoring from former students of mine.

A former student shared a story of how he was in a dispute with his wife over one of his daughter's boyfriends. The wife wanted him to tell the boyfriend to get lost. My student decided to defuse the situation, so while his wife was getting ready to go up the stairs, he put on some music they played at their wedding.

He goes on to say the strangest thing happened. As the songs were playing, she stopped, turned around, and said, "I guess it's OK for her to date this guy." He asked her what brought this on. She replied, "When that music came on, my mind flashed back to our wedding (many years ago) where Mother walked up to me and said, 'I still don't like him.' And you turned out all right."

That music fired an anchor installed many years before. But that is not the end of the story.

A few months later he took his wife for a getaway weekend on their anniversary. He broke out all the right anchors, flowers, champagne, the works! As soon as they settled in, he put on the same music as above. His wife stops, grabs him by the shoulders, stares into his eyes, and says, "Promise me something, we will not talk about our daughter or her boyfriends, or anything like that." He was blown away! Then he remembered that the last time he played this music, they were involved in an emotional experience. Because this new emotional experience was overlaid on the old anchor, it brought up the last "anchored" experience.

This is especially powerful when combined with rapport skills, calibration, and representational systems.

Here is another story from a student that puts the power of this into perspective. It is from retired master sergeant Robert Labrie and tells about the first time he put all these skills together when he was on assignment. He was part of the inspection team troubleshooting the Advertising and Promotion section.

> When I first arrived the supervisor said, "Sergeant Labrie, I am so glad to SEE you! I am so anxious to SHOW you how we run our Advertising and Promotion Program."
>
> He then spent time SHOWING me various slides, programs, and manuals he had written. He used visual terms. I knew that to please him, things had to look good.
>
> Then the officer in charge of the section approached me and said, "Sergeant Labrie, I am so anxious to HEAR what you have to SAY." She wanted clear, detailed explanations of everything I was covering during the inspections. I remember thinking that it can't be this easy (but it is!).
>
> I then met the third person. At first I couldn't make out his system, but then I noticed that every time I found something wrong, he would get very emotional and put his hand to his chest like I had stabbed him, and say, "I can't believe that there is so much wrong here, I FEEL like it will take me forever to get this all fixed." There were definite signs of him experiencing the world through primarily kinesthetic eyes.
>
> I would then match each of their language patterns, and I got along with each of them, but I could SEE how they had trouble in their communications with each other.
>
> I had an eighteen-page checklist to get through, and if the kinesthetic continued with the emotional outbursts, I would never complete it, so I decided to try "anchoring" for the first time. I asked him if he had ever been super successful in his life; he immediately said "yes." I asked him to

describe it in detail. The more he talked, the more I could SEE him get into a positive "state." His face was flushed; he began to talk faster and became more excited. When I thought it was the right moment (just before peak, bell curve) I grabbed his shoulder (kind of slapped it lightly) and said, "See, I told you, you could easily be successful, didn't I?"

He said "yes" and we proceeded to the next question, which also happened to be in an area that he needed work in. When I mentioned this fact, he went off again, just like before, except this time I slapped his shoulder, and before I could say a word, he said, "I know, I know, I was successful before, I can be successful again." I think my jaw hit the ground, it couldn't be that powerful, could it!

We went on to the next questions until we found another area that needed work and he began to fly off the handle again. Once again, all I needed to do was touch his shoulder, and he went into a positive state and said, "I know, I know," and we were off to the next question. After a while, all I had to do was approach him and look like I was going to touch his shoulder and he responded the same way.

I think it was then I became a true believer in the effectiveness of this technology, at that moment.

These are great examples of the many ways an anchor can be used—an association, a touch, a sound—to trigger a consistent response in your client. You can use anchors to tap into your customer's memory and imagination and transfer their positive feelings and associations to the present situation.

Think about some of the anchors you have. Do you have a certain song that causes you to feel a certain way? What happens when you see the national flag? What happens when your boss touches you on your shoulder and says, "I need to see you in my office"? Once you become comfortable with the idea of anchoring, why not use it to your advantage?

When you master rapport, you have a jump-start on friendly anchors. You must remember to be aware to anchor any positive states in your clients to you. You want to bring up those positive thoughts and feelings in your client's mind.

Once you become anchored to a response, it will last until changed or replaced by another anchor. This is true for people, products, or ideas. Here are some examples:

Coors beer invented light beer years before Miller brought out Miller Lite, but Miller anchored lite beer to them. Remember "Tastes Great, Less Filling"?

There were at least five gold rock-n-roll records before Elvis, but who is the King of Rock-n-Roll?

Do you ever hear someone say, "I need to make a Xerox of this?" Then they make a copy on a different brand copy machine.

What correct positive anchoring does is give you that unique mental spot in your customer's mind. You want them to think, "I need office products. I better give George a call. I like doing business with George."

Whenever I teach a class, the first thing I do is anchor the group. I like to anchor humor, or laughter, to myself. Every time the group laughs, I will touch my tie or face, in a certain way. I will then anchor spots on the stage. (Elite presenters talk about training their audience.)

I had a teacher in middle school, Mr. Stevens, who used to tutor a few of the students after class. One of his students, John, had a hard time coming up with the right answer to a question when called upon to do so in class. Mr. Stevens began to tutor him, and then, during class, he would ask a question and, before calling upon a student to answer, he would remark casually, "I know John has the answer to this question, but let's hear what Karen (or Tim, Mary, etc.) has to say." The result was that John started to believe in himself, that he had the answer. Mr. Stevens anchored a feeling of confidence in John that was reflected in the ease with which he began volunteering to answer questions in class.

Here are some exercises to master these skills. The first one is for you to practice on yourself. We want you to first get a feel for these techniques, and then we will show you how to implement them into your daily work and personal life.

Exercise: Anchoring a Resourceful State

Identify a resourceful state or behavior. Think of something you already do well, some behavior or state you would like to be able to access whenever you choose.

Choose an anchor that is easy for you to remember, that you can use whenever you want to access this feeling. Be sure to pick an anchor that is precise, such as placing your thumb and forefinger together as if making the "OK" sign.

Now call up a memory of the behavior or state you would like to have, remembering a time when it was strong. What was it like to be doing that behavior? It is important you see this experience through your own eyes, and not as if you are an observer watching yourself. Take note of what you see and hear and feel as you call up the memory. What colors are around you? Are the colors bright and vivid, or are they soft pastels? Are they clear, or are they slightly hazy and out of focus? What sounds do you hear? Are they soft or loud? Is there singing or talking or birds chirping? As you imagine this scene, allow yourself to experience being there until the feeling is strong and encompassing you. As you do, touch your thumb and forefinger together as if making the sign for "OK." Hold the position for as long as the feelings remain strong, and when they begin to fade, return your fingers to a relaxed position. Shake your head or move in some way so you can bring yourself back to the present (also called "breaking state").

The OK sign has just become the anchor for those feelings. But we don't want to stop there. In order to ensure these feelings are associated with that gesture, it is necessary to repeat the exercise a few more times. Each time you do, try to add more details to the memory. This makes it even more powerful. Use all of your senses (seeing, hearing, feeling, smelling, tasting) with the experience, so the connection between the memory and the anchor becomes powerful. It is important to remember anchors should be set (installed) at the peak of the experience. The purpose of setting the anchor is to be able to call up the desired state when needed.

Test the anchor. Think of a different experience and make the OK sign as you do, the same way you did a few minutes ago. This is known as firing the anchor. What happened? Did you recall the memory in all its detail, complete with the feeling or state you were trying to recapture? If you didn't, keep trying. Sometimes a little practice is all that is needed. Remember, the sensations in an experience will often rise and fall, so you want to set the anchor as the experience is reaching its peak and remove it when the feeling begins to fade.

Now that you are starting to understand the power of these techniques, here are some exercises to build your skills with others.

Some of the states you will want to learn how to anchor in others are:

- Humor
- Curiosity
- Being Positive
- Self-Confidence
- Loyalty
- How You Feel When You Make a GOOD Decision
- How You Feel When You Make a BAD Decision
- Excitement
- Doubt
- Patience

Eliciting States

Once you are in rapport with someone, you will find talking to them is easy. To get someone into the state you desire, you need to be able to elicit that emotional state in them. That may sound scary, but it is as natural as getting someone to talk about something that will put him or her in the state you want to elicit.

Here is an example you've probably come across: Two men start talking about their favorite sports team. As they talk, you can watch them enter into several emotional states. As they describe the last win, they get excited; they get passionate about the plays. Watch them as they describe a "bad call"—they get angry. If their team lost, you will see negative feelings.

In fact, watch any sporting event and you will see the athletes firing off anchors all the time. Maybe you played sports in school and you can still remember how you felt when you came off the field after a bad play and your coach gave you that look, or the excitement after a good play and your teammates patting you on the back

Another example before we move on to exercises. Watch a professional comic as they do their routine. If they have been on the road for a while, you will watch them set anchors in their audience if a joke goes well.

Think of the late Rodney Dangerfield. As he said his "I get no respect, no respect at all," he always touched his tie.

Jay Leno shrugs his shoulders on bad jokes, and that will get laughs. He touches his tie on good jokes.

Tim Allen used to make his grunting noises as he talked about power tools, and he built that into a multimillion-dollar TV career. You will even see him use similar gestures in some of his movies that have nothing to do with the TV show.

The secret to elicit a state in someone is that first you have to enter into it yourself! So if you want someone to be excited about something, you have to get excited yourself.

How do you do that? Think about something that makes you feel the way you want to feel. This will cause you to enter into the desired state. Then describe it in detail (even if just to yourself). Then ask the person with whom you are talking to describe how that state feels to them. If they hesitate, or have problems, just describe how you feel when you are in that state. People will compare, subconsciously, with how they feel when they are in that state.

Remember, when you are in rapport, people talk about a lot of things—this is natural; use it!

Anchoring States Exercises

Every day pick a state you will practice anchoring. We suggest coworkers and social situations before you tackle clients. Always start by getting into rapport with the people you are communicating with.

Humor. This does not mean you have to be a comic. Just get your target to talk about something they find funny, or anything that made them laugh. Start by telling a story you find amusing (I suggest you stay away from jokes, unless you're really good at them). If you are in rapport, they will start to smile with you. Then get them to talk about something they found amusing. As they describe it, and they smile or laugh, anchor that state to yourself by something. Touch your ear and smile or laugh with them. Repeat several times. When you touch your ear they will smile and be in a better mood.

Curiosity. This one is easy! Think about how you feel when you are curious. As you enter that state, do you touch your chin? (This seems to be a natural curiosity anchor.) Get your target to talk about things that make them curious. As they describe it, touch your chin.

Being Positive. A powerful state for anybody to use, on yourself, your coworkers, and your clients. Think about how you feel when you are in a positive state of mind, body, and spirit. Anchor that. Get your targets to enter into a positive state. When they are in that state, anchor it to yourself and to them. Anchor it to yourself by touching your chest area and maybe a thumbs-up sign. Anchor it to them with a pat on the shoulder.

Self-Confidence. Another winner for you and those around you. These are best when you find people in this state naturally, like after a good day, a good review at work, etc. I would anchor it with the same anchor as above.

The next ones will put you light years ahead of your competition.

Loyalty. This is one that will keep your clients around. Have them tell you something that they are loyal to, and how good they feel about being loyal. As they describe it, agree with them and anchor it to you with a natural movement such as running your hand through your hair. The key is how they feel when they are loyal—that's what you want. This is their way to ensure long-term relationships, as long as you live up to your part of the deal.

How They Feel When They Have Made a Good Decision. Yes, you get your target to talk about a good decision, and anchor that to you or your product. As they describe how they felt, you agree and anchor that to yourself or your product for them.

How they felt when they made a bad decision. As they talk about this, anchor this to your competition, or at least point away from you as they talk about it. This is powerful!

Excitement. Get your target to talk about anything that gets them excited. Sports, their kids—anything that puts them into excitement phase. You want to anchor this to your voice if possible. This will get them to take your calls and talk to you.

Doubt. Another winner for the salesperson. When you anchor in doubt, when they bring up objections, you can use this to steer them toward making a good decision!

Patience. This could be a deal saver if you need to get some extra time for the products or project. Anchor the feeling of patience your target has wanted from their clients on something, and how good they feel when their clients had patience with them. The key here is how they felt when someone had patience with them.

Here is a story that shows many of these in action.

> I was at a conference when someone approached me about buying some of my home study courses. I promptly put my rapport skills into practice. I mirrored and matched him. After he asked me about the home study courses, I told him how excited I was to be at the conference and that excitement is contagious. I asked him if he was excited, and as he went into saying how excited he was, I touched my tie.
>
> I then talked about how much fun it was just being here and laughing with my peers. I asked him if he was having a good time. As he described a funny event, I touched his shoulder and again touched my tie.

I asked him what he was curious about in the courses. As he told of his curiosity and fascination with NLP, I touched my chin and readily agreed (which I do).

We then talked about some of the good courses he had taken and which he was glad he did (good decision). As he was speaking of his favorite, I touched the home study courses.

I asked if he had been to any bad or unfulfilling things at the conference. As he described a couple, I made a gesture with my hand and talked about wasting time and money.

Now I had what I needed. I used his magic words, and I talked about how the home study courses were both fun and exciting; I touched my tie. He smiled.

I then talked about how this course answered all those questions about NLP many people in our field have; I touched my chin and his shoulder.

We then talked about how it was important to take good-quality courses and how you want your money's worth and to feel fulfilled. I touched the videotapes and held them.

I then talked about how there were other products and courses out there, and I did the gesture with my hand—he bought all of my courses.

Now I have to say I totally believe in these courses. They deliver the goods, so I was very passionate about that, and I wanted him to make a good decision.

As I was writing up the sale, I asked him about any special hobbies he had. He told me he loved to scuba dive. Great! Now we had a shared passion. He then mentioned he learned in the NAVY. I asked him if he liked his Navy experience. He said he loved it.

As he was talking about his love for the NAVY and his loyalty to it, I gave him the information on our organization, and how it feels to "be on board." As he was leaving, I stressed, "Welcome aboard the NFNLP ship."

He brought two other people over that weekend, one of whom bought a course. Is this stuff cool or what? By the way, he is a great NLP practitioner.

One last story. I was called in to consult with someone who did hypnosis seminars and wanted to sell more products in the back of the room, mainly tapes and books. I watched his presentation and recommended a few minor adjustments, the most powerful being as follows:

First, I had him place the products up front so they could be seen. Then as he talked about the great things the subconscious mind can do, I had him place his hand next to the products.

The focus was on when he pointed out the things the subconscious mind can do, that you want, that you need. He casually would gesture to the products.

For example, when he talked about how once you learn how to ride a bike, your mind will remember. You may not ride a bike for years, but when you get on one, your mind takes over and does it for you. This is a good thing, you want this, you need this (point to product) to free your attention to do other things. Another example is if you used to drive a stick shift. Again, you may not drive one for years, but then if you do within a few minutes, you're driving just fine. This you want, this you need (casually point to products). It's a good thing.

Then when he did his closing and talked about the products, he would say, "Some people need this, others want this, but what these do is free your mind. It's a good thing," as he held up the products. His sales went up over 10 percent at the next seminar.

Anchoring—a universal event: You can't NOT be anchored!

You are anchoring all the time in ways you are not even aware of. Anchoring is considered to be subliminal seduction, and is indeed a very powerful tool.

Anchoring Exercise

Ask someone to help you with the following exercise:

1. Identify resourceful behavior or state: Think of something you already do well, some behavior or state that is already resourceful, but which you would like to do even better.
2. Access and anchor number 1: What is it like to be doing that behavior? As they access that state, reach over and anchor it with a touch of the arm.
3. Identify additional resource number 2: Think of some other resource state/behavior that you could add so that you'd be even more delighted with that resourceful behavior. As they access this resource, anchor it with a touch of the other arm.
4. Integration: Take this resource (fire anchor number 2) and relive that resourceful behavior (fire anchor number 1) with this additional resource available to you. Watch and listen to everything that happens as these two experiences combine to make you even more effective. Take the time you need and come on back.
5. Test: Fire anchor number 1 and look for a new response.

Note: Anchors should be set at just before the peak of the experience. Have the client use all senses (seeing, hearing, feeling, smelling, and tasting) that were associated with the experience. Ask the client to nod when they have reached the peak of the experience. Then set the anchor. The purpose of setting the anchor is to be able to call up that particular desired state when needed.

The next time you do this, how will it be different? And you fire the first anchor. You want them to go in and sort all differences. So what's it like? It may only be one subtle shift.

Remember you are anchoring people all the time. Think about all the times you might touch someone on the shoulder and say, "It's OK! How bad is it?" And you set an anchor every time. They get anchored into "this is feel bad time."

In the old Gestalt therapy, the therapist would start in one chair, and as the patient got better, he'd go to another chair and could not go back to the old chair because that was the bad chair. "You are better now, you can't sit there anymore." They were anchoring and didn't know what it was.

Some trainers covertly install humor throughout their presentation to make the class more interesting. It especially helps when you make a mistake. You can tap while you are creating the anchor. You can use your voice. Using a middle name, such as "William Danny Horton," immediately reminds you of a time when you were getting chewed out by your mom. You can anchor in the air with a gesture. You feed back their strategy and add an anchor. A trainer can anchor his/her spaces on the stage so that whenever he/she steps into a certain area or does a certain thing, the audience will react in a certain way. Stand in a certain spot when you tell a story. Anchoring makes all your techniques more powerful.

Exercise: Altering an Action/Behavior Transfer

Presenter (P): Does anyone have a problem or a time in their life when they get stuck or have a response they don't like and can't get out?

    a. It doesn't hurt to use the book. It means there will be less you have to remember.

    b. Presumably, if a doctor has a question, he will go to a manual to get the answer.

    c. Grab the book if you need to.

P: You start to make a decision and you get stuck. Where do you get stuck? What happens for you to get stuck? . . . Do you think about it a long time? . . . Do you think too much?

Experiencer (E): I think too much. I analyze it.

P: Would you like to stop doing that to a certain degree?

P: Please close your eyes and we will be doing anchoring with touch—if you don't mind?

P: Can you see yourself from my point of view? Like on a movie screen? See yourself so you are totally dissociated? There is no feeling, no thought. Now shake that off.

P: Can you think of the last time you got stuck? When was that? What was it? What were you thinking about?

E: The change I was going to make.

P: OK! Think about that now! And you know how it feels to be stuck. Right? You know how it feels mentally and physically.

P: Now what I want you to do, have your brain do this . . . From now on whenever you get stuck, you are automatically going to pull back and see yourself from my point of view. Got it?

P: So when you think about being stuck, you are going to pull back and see yourself from my point of view.

P: Shake that off and open your eyes. So how is it different now when you think about being stuck?

P: Pull back. What resource, that is what we are looking for, and we just tested it. That in itself can be an intervention if you are dealing with people. So what can happen is they get stuck and they don't get out of it. And sometimes just by pulling back it can be an intervention.

Have you ever worked with someone who gets into an "instant rage?" They just flip from being normal to being insane, and sometimes all they need is someone to pull them back. If they can pull back and see themselves in rage, they usually will regain control.

So what resource would be handy for you to have when you are stuck? What do you think would be good? You get stuck in that think . . . think . . . think . . . think . . . think and you pull back . . . what would be good? Go ahead and trust your instinct—yes, go ahead and do it.

Just shut the faucet off and go. OK, we can do that.

Steps to Behavior Transfer

1. Can you think of a time when you could do that, just shut the faucet off and go? Yes!

2. Enter that now and think about it. So you know what that is like?
3. OK? So from now on, here is what is going to happen!
   Whenever you start getting stuck, you are automatically going to pull back and see yourself sitting there stuck . . . and when you settle back in it, you will maybe just shut the faucet off and go.
4. But it is going to happen—stuck, pull back, and all of a sudden you are just ready to go.
5. Stuck, pull back, ready to go. Before you know it, it will happen faster than I could touch you.
6. So the next time you start getting stuck . . . snap your fingers . . . it's done!
7. Now just to make this even more fun, I want you to take your left hand and either make a fist or an OK sign or do something with your left hand . . . an OK sign.
8. That's going to be your anchor. So if something happens and you get stuck and it doesn't happen automatically, just by doing the OK sign, this will automatically happen.
9. So you might even make the OK sign, your self-anchor, when you know you've got to make a decision. So you start making that OK sign and your brain automatically goes, "OK, let's just go!"
10. Always know you can trust yourself to make the best decision at the time. So this becomes your self-anchor for that.

Solicit the help of another person and review the previous exercise

Have them think of a time that they get stuck or they go into an unresourceful state. Find something that they get some type of stimulus from, but whose response they don't like.

Examples: Rage

My wife just says something to me and I go off . . . stimulus/response.
Every time my husband comes home, he leaves his clothes on the floor, takes a shower . . . it drives me crazy. Stimulus/response.

1. Have them elicit dissociation
   Give them a safety valve if something goes wrong . . . you want them to be able to dissociate.
   Ask them if they can see themselves from my point. Picture yourself on a movie screen.
   See yourself from the top of the room, whatever you want so they can imagine themselves being dissociated. (Set anchor number 1 wherever it is handy for you—knee, elbow, etc).
   Precise, exact spot is not necessary. Close is good enough.

2. Test it, then elicit the stuck state . . . Have them think about the last time it happened when they got stuck (anchor number 2).

3. Chain to dissociation: From now on, whenever you feel yourself getting stuck, angry, upset, losing control, whatever the problem the client has . . . you automatically find yourself pulling back (or dissociated) or "drift back and see yourself getting angry," or something like that.

    Note: Always do everything twice.

4. Test: Have the client think about being stuck and usually they will go . . . their eyes will go all over the place. You have scattered the neurology of the brain.

5. Then ask them to select a resource—What would be good . . . ? He said, "Turning the faucet off and going." (Anchor it.)

6. Then tie all three anchors together—From now on, not only when you feel stuck will you automatically pull back and see yourself, you are also going to settle into turning the faucet off and go.

They could say humor versus the faucet, for example.

Don't give advice. Find out what resource they need, and no matter how weird it sounds, use it. It has to be their idea. For them it might be humor and a pile of clothes. One person would just pick the clothes up, throw them in the closet and go on, or just leave them there. Let them come up with whatever works in their brain.

Now if they obviously don't know, then prod them, but it is important to let them put it in their words. That is easy to overlook. That is why psychology has a dismal track record. We take what works with one person and think it will work with everyone.

You overlap the patterns in the brain. Anchors can override other anchors depending on the strength of the stimulus—like taping over a tape.

Eliminating Fears and Phobias

This technique neutralizes the powerful negative feelings of phobias and traumatic events.

Remember, most people learned to be phobic in a single situation that was actually dangerous or seemed dangerous. The fact that individuals can do what psychologists call "one-trial learning" is proof that a person's brain can learn quite rapidly. That ability to learn rapidly makes it easy for you to learn a new way to respond to any phobia or trauma.

The part of you that has been protecting you all these years by making you phobic is an important and valuable part. We want to preserve its ability to protect you in dangerous situations. The purpose of this technique is to refine and improve your brain's ability to protect you by updating the information.

Have the subject get comfortable. Following are questions and a suggested patter for this technique.

- What is your phobia?
- Do you want to be over it?
- How bad is your phobia? What happens?
- And you would like to be over this?
- First thank your brain for a couple of things. (1) It proves how quickly your brain works. (2) Once it learns something, it can be tenacious.
- Intellectually you know that most snakes are not poisonous, but that doesn't matter . . . does it?
- Thank your brain for holding onto this for all these years. And it's doing it for some reason to take care of you.
- All we are going to do is update the information collected by your brain. OK?
- What I want you to do is put your feet flat and just close your eyes, and I want you to imagine you are sitting in a movie theatre in your favorite chair, and on the screen is a great big black-and-white snapshot of you, where everything is fine. You got it?
- Now what I want you to do is float out of your body so you can see yourself sitting in the chair. And you are going to drift back up like where the projection booth would be, and you are going to see yourself sitting here safe and secure, watching yourself watch the movie.
- So you are up in the projection booth, and there is plastic up there, and you are safe and totally removed, and you are up here watching yourself sitting here watching the movie.
- Got it? Good! Now I want you to watch and listen . . . protected in this booth as you see this black-and-white snapshot kind of segue into a movie of a younger you going through one of those situations where you experienced a phobia reaction with [phobia].
- It might be the earliest memory you can remember, or it could be the worst, either one. But you are up here in the projection booth watching yourself, safe and secure, sitting there watching this movie . . . as it goes from a black-and-white snapshot into a black-and-white movie of you either the very first time you freaked out with [name phobia] or the worst time you freaked out with [name phobia].
- And the movie is going to run all the way through the end and it stops. And there's a black-and-white picture of you again at the end, and everything is fine.
- Now what you are going to do for me is you are going to drift out of the projection booth and you are going to settle back down into your body, safe and secure, and when you are ready, you are going to take a deep, deep breath . . . hold it . . . take another deep breath and hold it.
- You are going to step into that last picture, and the whole movie is going to run backward and in color. *Swoooosh!* Just like that—real fast all the way back to the beginning, that's right!

- Now come out of the movie, come back and sit down, safe and secure. Drift up out of your body again and see yourself sitting here and again the movie is going to start over.
- Again, the very first time or the very worst time you had an experience with a snake all the way through to the end, it freezes. You drift out of the movie theatre into yourself, and whenever you are ready on your own you are going to take a deep breath, step into the movie, and as you exhale, the movie is going to run backward and in color, with you in it.
- See, hear, and feel everything as it goes backward . . . *swoosh*, like that. Got it?
- This time you don't even go back to the projection booth; you just come sit down here and watch the movie. This time it is in color, of the worst experience you ever had with a snake, but you are watching it . . . swoosh all the way to the end. When you step into it, the movie runs backward and in color . . . *swoosh* . . . real quick! OK?
- And then it ends and you come back out and you see a huge picture, one of those forty-foot pictures, like the old drive-in movie screen. There you are, being the person you really want to be!
- What I want you to realize is since you had this phobia you have [avoided your phobia and you haven't learned as much as you could have about the subject of your phobia], you'll know how to urge caution in your intelligence and your training . . . to be cautious and careful . . . and you may be surprised and delighted right now as you begin to search in vain for that phobic response.
- [Think of phobia in a smaller way—e.g., smaller snake, smaller spider, etc.] Whenever you are ready, open your eyes. How are you feeling?
- How do you think you would feel if [you experienced phobia now]?
- Thank your brain for understanding all this stuff and you are going to exercise caution, and so when you see [name phobia], don't run up and look at it, but you might go hmmmm . . . interesting!

CHAPTER 8

Information Gathering

Once you achieve rapport with a person or persons, you will find gathering information easier. They will want to talk to you, because they will feel a sense of connectedness.

At the very outset, you are advised to bear in mind that to gather the correct information, you will need to do more than just listen to their words. You will also need to decode their meaning. This is because we do not operate directly in the real world but have to create models, or maps of the world, which we then use to direct our behavior. These maps or models allow us to make sense of the world and of all our experiences.

Now, the maps or models in question cannot be evaluated in terms of good or bad, but only in terms of their ability to help us cope with the world. Most of us create these models from three human language modeling processes, namely, **deletion**, **distortion**, and **generalization**. These are what allow us to grow, understand, and experience the world.

The most common of these is **generalization**. This is where a person takes pieces or parts of an experience and uses it to represent the whole category from which that experience is but an example. A child learns his father is a male, and he generalizes this and believes all males become daddies. This is also how you can learn quickly. For instance, when you learn how to drive a car, you can generalize what you learn about driving a car so you can drive almost any automobile.

However, generalization has its limitations. For example, when a salesperson fails in a few calls, or performs in a way he labels inadequate, he or she could generalize this into believing that they are no good at sales calls.

The next process is **distortion**. This is where we make shifts in how we experience our sensory data. We misrepresent reality, sometimes making it more or less important than it really is. People who do this because they are optimists are said to be looking at the world through rose-colored glasses. The other side of the coin, however, can become a problem, such as when someone takes a small amount of criticism from his sales manager and turns it into "He hates me and is out to get at me."

It can also be a problem when someone takes a process and turns it into a thing. Love becomes something to be handled, and controlled, as if it was a thing.

Lastly we have **deletion**. This is where someone leaves out certain aspects of an experience and focuses on other aspects, somewhat like selective attention. On the plus side this allows you not to become overwhelmed by all the external stimuli you are confronted with daily—you can talk on the cell phone while walking through the airport, oblivious to all the hustle around you.

Victim mentality can be an example of this. Such a person believes the world is against him, but he deletes his actions, which may have put him into such a position or caused his problems in the first place.

Here is a complete breakdown of the language process we call the meta model. Read through this, and then I will show you a way to cut to the chase, so to speak.

Meta Model Distinctions

People have their own system for connecting words to their daily experiences, and their own set of words to help connect to that experience. People are usually not conscious of the process or the words they select to represent their experience.

Errors in information gathering can be divided into two types:

1. *Deletions*—information that was lost as you represented the words given to you by the customer.
2. *Additions*—information that you added to that representation, based on your own presuppositions, personal history, etc.

What do we mean when we speak of deletions and additions? Well, deletion occurs when we selectively focus on certain parts of our experience and exclude other parts. It's something we all do almost all the time to avoid being overwhelmed by the external stimuli that surround us. For instance, someone in a room full of people can play a video game, while another person is watching television and three other people are playing a board game. Each person in that room is deleting a portion of the total experience in order to engage in their selected activity.

How does deletion occur when we are with a customer? Imagine that you have just asked your customer a question about their computer software preference. The customer replies, describing his use of certain software and his inability to get technical help when he needs it. As a computer salesperson with a background in programming, you have never experienced his level of frustration. You focus on the software he mentioned and talk about how versatile these applications can be. You have unconsciously deleted his technical-help problems, without even realizing that you did so.

Addition occurs when we add something to a representation based on our own experience. Take the above example. This time the salesperson recalls a time when he called for technical help with a software application and spoke with a troubleshooter who gave him some insightful tips about the application. He misses the frustration being expressed by his customer because he is concentrating on his own memory and recalling how knowledgeable the technician was and how he was able to use the tips to greatly increase his expertise with the software application. The original representation of the customer, that his use of certain software programs led to seeking technical help that was less than helpful, is distorted by the salesperson's own experience.

The Meta Model is a set of questions that allows you to gather information that clarifies someone's experience, in order to get a full and detailed representation of that experience. The goal of the Meta Model is to create the most understanding and learning from any specific communication.

The Meta Model is used to gather information that leads a person from a surface structure, SS (the language selected to represent an experience), to a deep structure, DS (the actual, complete experience).

There are seven question-words in the English language: *who, what, when, where, how,* and *why.* Of these, *why* is the only one that doesn't ask for specific detail. The answer to "Why?" is usually "Because," followed by a historical or theoretical explanation, in contrast to the process information you want. You may get specific detail in response to "Why?" but that will only be a lucky accident. This is why the question "Why?" does not appear in the Meta-Model.

Meta Model responses help recover deleted material and assist the speaker in reconnecting with their deep structure (the actual, complete experience). This can be the most important part of a sales call, namely, gathering the correct information.

Gathering Information

Lack of Referential Index

When the person or thing being referred to is not identified, this is known as lack of referential index. This type of generalization limits your model of the world by leaving out the specific details of the experience or representation. These references are often pronouns, such as *she, he, it, they, them,* and classes of objects, such as dogs, hotels, cars, countries, etc. When you are gathering information from a customer, you want to be sure that you have a clear understanding of what they are saying. The details that they leave out can make or break the sale.

1. **Deleted Referential Index** is where the speaker of the sentence simply leaves out the reference.

    A. *"The window was broken."*
       Who broke it?
    B. *"I'm being pushed into this project."*
       Who's pushing you?

2. **Unspecified Referential Index** occurs when the noun or noun phrase does not name a specific person or thing . . . words like "this," "that," and "it"—

    A. *"That just won't work."*
        What specifically won't work?
    B. *"This is stupid."*
        What is stupid?

3. **Generalized Referential Index** is one way the speaker can "plug the hole" left by deleting a reference. A generalized referential index is a noun or pronoun which refers to a nonspecific group or category.

    A. *"Relationships are a drain."*
        Which relationships do you find draining?
    B. *"People are so uncaring."*
        Who specifically is so uncaring?

4. **Reversed Referential Index** occurs when the speaker is stated as receiving the action of the verb in a sentence rather than doing the action of the verb.

    A. *"He hates me."*
        Try saying "I hate him," and then express what you're feeling.
    B. *"She never seems to understand me."*
        Try saying, "I never seem to understand her," and then express what exactly you're feeling.

The creator of the Gestalt theory, Fritz Perls, called this linguistic pattern projection. As people begin to take responsibility for themselves in this manner, they have the possibility of having an "Aha!" experience. This is referred to as owning projection.

Nominalizations

This Referential Index Meta-Model violation has its own category. Nominalizations are words transformed from process (verbs) into closed events (nouns).

Change the noun or constant state back into an active form of the verb from which it was derived. Specifically ask "who" or "what."

Open up the action.
Who's communicating what to whom?
How would you like to communicate?

Linguistically, nominalizing is the changing of a DS process into an SS event.

Ask yourself the question: "Can you put the nominalization in a wheelbarrow?" or does the word fit into the blank of the syntactic frame: "Ongoing . . . ?"

Words like *friendship, sensation, decision, obligation,* etc. are nominalizations.

You need to denominalize the words.

Questions to ask:
"How specifically are you . . . ?"
"What prevents you . . . ?"
"Can you imagine . . . ?"

A. *"He is a failure."*
   How is he failing?

B. *"This relationship is not working out."*
   How is the way you are relating not working out for you?

C. *"I can't do anything without being reminded of my obligations."*
   To whom are you obligated to do what?

D. *"My wife's laughter provokes my anger."*
   How does your wife's laughing cause you to feel angry?

E. *"I resent your question."*
   How (what) do you resent in what (that) I am asking you?

Unspecified Verbs

In an Unspecified Verb, a full description of the action or event is not present.

Question to ask:
How specifically?

To say that someone touched me is much more generalized than to say someone caressed me.

A. *"Michelle rejects me."*
   How specifically does Michelle reject you?

B. *"They ignore me."*
   How specifically do they ignore you?

C. *"He hurts me."*
   How specifically does he hurt you?

D. *"John keeps bothering me."*
   How specifically does John keep bothering you?

Note that the above statements also include a Reversed Referential Index.

Expanding Limits

Modal Operators of Possibility/Necessity (Modes of Operation) are words that identify the limitations a person puts on him/herself.

Possibility/Impossibility: can/can't; will/won't; possible/impossible.

Necessity (Required): should/shouldn't; must/must not; necessary/unnecessary.

These operators define the boundaries of the person's model of the world. To extend beyond those boundaries is to invite some catastrophic expectation over which the speaker believes he/she has no control.

Questions to ask:
   What stops you?
   What would happen if you did?

1. *"I can't do that."*
   What would stop you?
   What would you do if you did?

2. *"I won't be able to go to the concert alone."*
   What stops you from going to the concert alone?
   What do you think would happen if you went alone?

3. *"I really should be more flexible."*
   What do you think would happen if you were more flexible?

4. *"I ought to be more understanding when he's like that."*
   What do you think would happen if you weren't?

5. *"It's not possible for me to love anymore."*
   What stops you from loving?
   What would happen if you did?

Must, have to, ought to, and their opposites, shouldn't, must not.

Universal Quantifiers

With Universal Quantifiers, everything is exaggerated. This category includes words such as *all, never, always, no one* and *everybody*. They often indicate that a generalization has been made from a specific experience.

The question to ask should be in the form of an exaggeration. Ask for contradictions to the event the speaker is talking about.

1. *"I never get what I want."*
   Can you think of a time when you did get what you wanted?

2. *"No one will give me help."*
   I wonder if you can remember at least one person who helped you?

3. *"Everybody's mean to me."*
   Everybody's always mean to you, everyone you know, even your best friend, even the milkman?

4. *"I've always used the wrong words."*
   You've always used the wrong words at every time and in every situation?

Universal Quantifiers often have built-in double binds.

"Though I want to, I'll never respect him . . . I always get what I want from him." I have a homework assignment for you. During the coming week I would like you to ask him to give you only what you want in order to respect him.

Mind Reading

Mind Reading is the belief on the part of someone that one person can know what another is thinking/feeling without direct communication (knowing someone's internal state).

Projected Mind Reading: a person believes that others should know what he/she is thinking.

Questions to ask:
How specifically do you know that?

1. *"I know what makes her happy."*
   How specifically do you know what makes her happy?

2. *"You love me."*
   How specifically do you know that I love you?

3. *"He should know better."*
   How should he know not to do that?

4. *"They think he knows all the answers."*
   How specifically do you know that they think that?

5. *"If she cared about me, she wouldn't have to ask what I need."*
   If she doesn't ask, then how will she know for sure what you need?

Changing Meanings

Cause and Effect

Cause and Effect is a belief that some action on the part of one person can cause another to experience emotion or an inner state, where cause is wrongly put outside of self.

Questions to ask:
How does X cause Y? How specifically?

1. *"Michael's nervousness causes me to be edgy."*
   How specifically does Michael's nervousness cause you to be edgy?

2. *"Reading this makes me angry."*
   How specifically?

3.   *"You make me sad."*
     How specifically?

4.   *"I feel bad for making her cry."*
     What did you do that you believe made her cry?

5.   *"Their laughter makes me angry."*
     How does their laughing cause you to be angry? (notice the nominalization in sentence number 5 . . . laughter)

Lost Performative

A Lost Performative is a generalization that a person makes and transfers to the world as if it is a truth. The personally held belief gets lost in the generalizations (value judgments where the person doing the judging is left out).

Questions to ask:
Who says? For whom?

1.   *"It's crude to act like that."*
     Who says?

2.   *"This is the right way to do this project."*
     According to whom?

3.   *"That's a stupid thing to do."*
     Stupid according to whom?

4.   *"It's not important anyway."*
     It's not important to whom?

By using Lost Performatives, people remove themselves from any position that might leave them open to criticism or challenge. "Statistically speaking . . ."

By getting the speaker to use such phrases as "I think" or "my belief is," the speaker is able to identify him/herself as the specific performer of the judgment, thought, belief, or action.

The Short Method

Now that you have an idea of how we use language to make sense out of the world and how we can lose the true meaning in these processes, let us show you a shortcut.

The thing to bear in mind is to get your customer (or anyone you are communicating with) to be as specific as possible. You want to elicit information that is as sensory-specific as possible—things you can SEE, HEAR, or TOUCH. When you do this, you will be communicating in a way that makes understanding much easier. The word(s) you now want to start using a lot:

Specific/Specifically

Now, when you first start this process, some people may be upset when you nail them down by requiring specificity, but you will also become known as a clear communicator. As a culture, we have lost clear communication and replaced it with the vague reference.

Here is a list of the key questions to learn to ask in almost any situation in which you want to gather clear information.

The Key Questions:

1) What do you want?
   Stated in positive terms
   Specific
   Sensory Based
   Hear
   Feel
1a) What will that do for you? (specifically)
2) How will you know when you have it?
3) Where, when, and with whom do you want it?
4) How will this affect other aspects (or people) in your life?
5) What stops you from having this already?
6) What resources do you already have that will help you obtain your outcome?
7) What additional resources do you need to obtain it?
8) How are you going to get there?
8a) First step: Must be specific and achievable.
   Is there more than one way to get there?

The Key to Successful Interaction
The Meta Model

We are going to talk about the meta model of information gathering. Meta means overview, huge, above. It is a way of gathering information specifically. After this exercise, you will fall in love with the word "specifically," and chances are that everyone around you will want to slap you.

We talk about getting upset, and often it is a person who makes us upset. Well, specifically, what are you upset about? How specifically does he/she upset you? People do not want specifics in their life. They want generalizations (fluff words).

The two ways to gather information:

1. You can go up to a more generalized term (fluffy language).
2. You can go down to something specific.

You should focus on what you can see, hear, and feel. For example, instead of saying, "I want to be happy," think what, specifically, will make you happy. How specifically do you know if you are happy?

Let us deal with some specific questions . . .

1) What do you want? Why are you reading this?
   Stated in positive terms, we are looking for a positive goal; not what you **don't** want.
   This is great if you work with people who want a relationship. Most people can tell you exactly what they don't want in a person, which is usually just like the person they just left or those qualities.
   I am not interested in what you don't want, but what you do want.

   Are you reading this for therapy or business?

   - Has to be in your realm of experience.
   - Specific—Sensory Based—See—Hear—Feel.
   - Small chunk size.

   Example: I want to kill my wife. I want to be a vegetarian. I want to stop smoking.
   It's a specific goal, initiated and controlled by the client.
   Ask yourself specifically "how are you going to do that."

2.) What will that do for you? (Specifically).

1) I will feel better.

2) Is there any other way you can feel better than killing your wife?

3.) How will you know when you have it?

   a. How will you see, hear, and feel?

4.) Where, when, and with whom do you want it?

Do you want this everywhere in your life, or is this a specific situation?

For example, if someone wanted to be more assertive in their life. Where, when, and with whom do you want to be more assertive, specifically? Home, kids, work? Is it sensory based and ecological? Make sure it is good for the whole system.

5.) How will this affect other aspects (or people) in your life?

Assertiveness, for example.

Let us consider the example of the lady who wanted to become a vegetarian. This decision isn't something that will affect the lady alone. The entire family may have to eat less meat.

Similarly, if a member of the family wants to quit smoking, it will mean that the whole family may have to smoke outside.

6.) What stops you from having this already?

7.) What resources do you have that will help you obtain the outcome you desire?

   a. Success in one area can be transferred to success in another.

8.) What additional resources do you need to obtain it?

9.) How are you going to get there?

   a. First step: Be specific and achievable. How will you start?
   b. Is there more than one way to get there?

The following story will help exemplify this point.

The Guru

There was this town that had a town Guru. He was a person who knew all the answers. Now, there was a family that was having a problem with their son. The son would eat chocolate and candy, get hyper, eat more candy, and go on until he was out of control.

After exhausting all their resources, they went to the Guru and told him of their problem. He told them to come back in two weeks, by which time, he said, he would have an answer for them.

Rumors spread about this Guru who was supposed to have all the answers immediately. Was he losing it?

Finally, the two weeks over, they went back to the Guru. He told them what to do, and it worked. All the elders of the town got together to find out why it took the Guru so long (two weeks) to get an answer.

They approached the Guru for a clarification. He said he had a problem with sweets; he got hyper, and would then pass out. He admitted that he hadn't realized it was a problem until they had presented it to him.

How could he help them with a problem that he himself had, until he had solved it for himself? So he went to his Guru to find out how to solve the problem.

Guru = Gee, you are you.

Now let us move on to a simple exercise on how to lose weight.

Exercise: How to lose weight:

(P) What is it specifically that you want?
(E) To lose weight.
(P) How much weight do you specifically want to lose?
(E) I want to get down to 110 lbs.
(P) What would that do for you?
(E) It would make me look better and feel better and fit in my clothes better.
(P) So you want to look better and feel better, and losing weight would do that for you?
(P) Are there any specific foods that are primarily giving you a problem?
(E) I am a sweetaholic.
(P) What types of sweets particularly?
(E) Candy, cookies, cake, and pie.
(P) When do you usually eat the sweets?
(E) I do well during the day, but when I get home—ah! That's when I lose it!
(P) So you want to eat better, salads, etc.? Did you ever eat that good?
(E) No!
(P) So this will be a new behavior for you?
(P) How will this affect other people in your life?
(E) They would like it.
(P) What stops you from already achieving your goal?
(E) I never learned to eat fruits and vegetables.

(P) What resources do you already have that will help you get there?
(E) Books, etc.; I have motivation, desire, programming.
(P) What additional resources do you need to obtain it?
(P) So you have taken these steps but something hasn't clicked?
(P) What is the next step you are going to take to get there?

When you communicate, it is normal to Distort—Generalize—Delete information, and it is usually the information that is left out that is most important.

Let us take a peek at what these are.

Distortions

1. Mind-Reading Pattern

   This is apparently knowing what someone else is thinking or feeling.

   Response: How do you know? You really don't know. They did it in the past. Past behavior is the best predictor for future behavior. Sounds good but doesn't mean anything. Always ask. Always probe. Always question. And never take anything for granted.

   Prediction: Recover source of information
   Another example: "I know you are upset with me." How do you really know?

2. Lost-Performative Pattern
   This is general semantics from Alfred Korzipski. It's about how language is processed. As we already learned, sentences have two structures: the deep structure and the surface structure.

   They are deleting what is being judged. It's bad to be inconsistent.

   Response: (Gather evidence) Who says it is bad? According to whom? How do you know? You have lost the performance factor. You need to focus on who or what is the performance thing you are doing.

   Prediction: Recover Source of Belief.
   Recover Performative
   Recover Belief Strategy

3. Cause-Effect Pattern
   "You make me sad."

   Response: How does what I am doing cause you to be sad? How do you know you are sad, specifically?
   Prediction: Recover choice.

4. Complex-Equivalents Pattern
   Two experiences being interpreted as being synonymous.
   "She's always yelling at me; she doesn't like me!"
   Response: Have you ever yelled at someone you liked? How does her yelling mean . . . ?
   You could be yelling because you just got a letter from the IRS. You have to break the equivalence.

   Prediction: Recover CEQ. Counterexample.

5. Presuppositions Pattern

   Example: If my husband knew how much I suffered, he wouldn't do that.

   Three Suppositions:

   (1) I suffer.
   (2) My husband acts in some way.
   (3) My husband doesn't know I suffer.

   Response:

   (1) How do you choose to suffer?
   (2) How is he reacting?
   (3) How do you know he doesn't know?

   You are presupposing he cares.
   By challenging it, you are breaking the other's model of the world.

   (1) Specify choice and verb.
   (2) Specify what he does.
   (3) Recover internal representation and CEQ.

Generalizations

6. Universal-Quantifiers Pattern
    (*all, every, never, everyone, no one,* etc.)
    Examples: She never listens to me!
                Everyone does everything.
                (Kids use this a lot.)
                Everyone is going to the dance.
                You have to do this/that.

    Challenge! What would happen if you did?

    Response: (find counterexamples) Never! What would happen if she did?
    Prediction: Recover counterexample effects, outcome.

7. Modal-Operators Pattern

    a. Modal Operators of Necessity (required)
        (*Should, shouldn't, must, must not, have to, need to, it is necessary*)
        Example: I have to take care of her.

        Response: What would happen if you did? What would happen if you didn't?
        Prediction: Recover effects, outcome.

    b. Modal Operators of Possibility (or impossibility)
        (*Can/can't, will/won't, may/may not, possible/impossible*)

        Example: I can't tell him the truth.

        Response: What prevents you? What would happen if you did?
        Prediction: Recover causes.

Deletions

8. Nominalizations Pattern (process words, verbs that have been turned into nouns)
    Turning a process or something nonconcrete into a concrete event.
        If you can't put it in a wheelbarrow . . . If you can't see it, feel it, or touch it, it
    is a nominalization.
        Example: "I'm in love." What does love look like? This is fun in communication
    because you find out if you are speaking the same language or not.

Response: Who's communicating what to whom? How would you like to communicate?

Prediction: Turn back into a process, recover deletion, and referential index. Process and specify verb.

9. Unspecified-Verbs Pattern

Example: "He rejected me."
People don't specify what's going on with them.

Response: How, specifically, did he reject you?
Prediction: Specify the verb.

10. Simple-Deletions Pattern

a. Simple Deletions. Example: "I am uncomfortable."
b. Lack of Referential Index. Example: "They don't listen to me."
(fails to indicate a specific person or thing)
c. Comparative Deletions. Example: "She's a better person."
(*good, better, best, more, less, most, least, worse, worst*)

Response:

a. About what, whom?
b. Who, specifically, doesn't listen to you?
c. Better than whom? Better than what? Compared to whom, what?

Prediction:

a. Recover Deletion
b. Recover Referential Index
c. Recover Comparative Deletion

CHAPTER 9

Calibration

Subconscious Communication, Level 1

To understand and communicate with another person's subconscious mind, it's necessary to review basic rapport and look a little more deeply at how the human mind, in theory, works. Once you've understood this, you can begin to see how successful people are able to bypass the critical factors of the mind.

The first thing you need to do to sharpen your skills is to learn how to focus on your target's communication style. You need to learn how to calibrate your targets or anyone you are communicating with. We've discussed communication styles, but now let's put it to practical application.

Here is a story that will illustrate calibration and rapport skills:

> I was on my way from Chicago to Newark on Memorial Day one year to speak at a conference when an opportunity to sharpen my skills in communication came my way. I got to the airport to find that I had missed my plane. Now, I do recollect that it was totally my fault. When I had got the tickets, I had not checked the timings closely. I thus thought the plane was scheduled to leave at 1:11, and when I got to the gate I discovered to my horror that the plane had already left at 11:11. Surprised, I checked the ticket, only to learn to my dismay that the ETD indicated on my ticket, though lightly, was indeed the correct time, namely, 11:11. I had misread it.
>
> I went to the ticket counter and found a long line, due to some weather problems; I fell in line and started thinking of how to get to the conference. My first reaction was to go on the offensive and point out the light printing. In fact, I was taking my self-anger and was externally focusing it on the situation.
>
> As the line got closer to the front, I could see the anger that the airline agents were being subjected to. Naturally they were very defensive. I realized that I needed another strategy to get my goal of getting to the conference without paying a huge amount. Right before I got to the front, I overheard that all the flights of this airline were full.

When it was my turn to approach the counter, I took a deep breath and walked up. I looked the agent in the eye. I saw she was tired and worn out. I slumped my shoulders and appeared tired, too.

"Looks like you're having a rough day," I said very tiredly.

"You would not believe it," she said ruefully.

I looked at the line as she did, saying, "Yeah, but do you work this weekend?"

"No, a couple of hours and I am out of here for the holiday."

"Well, keep that picture in your mind, and it may help you get through the rest of the day. Got any special plans?" I asked a split-second pause later, trying to get her to pull out of the situation and get into a better mood. I added energy to my speech and pulled my shoulders back.

"Yeah, I can't wait!" she smiled for the first time.

"Well I hate to admit this, but I really screwed up." I took out my ticket. "I hate to show you how silly I was (I paused)—did you ever make a stupid mistake?" I asked, hoping she would want to help.

"Oh, all the time! Let me see—I bet I have fouled up worse," she said as she took my ticket.

"Keep thinking of this weekend," I said as I handed her the ticket. Anchoring a positive.

"So you misread the ticket?" she asked.

"Yea, it was silly," I replied.

"Well it was hard to read—and all our flights are full," she replied.

"I was going to a conference this weekend, where I was to speak to a group of therapists and hypnotists. I guess I will miss it. Well, you keep thinking of this weekend with your family," I said, exhaling and looking down, going back to being tired.

"Sounds interesting. Let's see what we can do," she replied in an upbeat mood.

She spent a couple of minutes at her computer; then looking up she said brightly, "Get to the next terminal; I got you on a business flight on another airline! Hurry and have a good time!" She smiled as she handed me the new ticket. "Enjoy your conference" was her last comment.

"You keep your eyes on the weekend!" I said as I left the counter.

By pacing and calibrating to the ticket agent's state, I was able to establish a rapport with her and led her into a better state, a state in which I was able get her to want to help me.

You experience the world by collecting information through your five senses and processing it internally. The five primary senses are visual, auditory, kinesthetic, gustatory (taste), and olfactory (smell). As input from your five senses is processed by your brain, it is translated into corresponding internal representations, or maps, that create a likeness of the real world.

So through your eyes, ears, and sense of touch, taste, and smell, you make contact with the world, what is called reality. However, it isn't so much what is out there; it's the things you see, hear, touch, taste, and smell which fill your everyday experience. It is the maps of reality inside your head—your beliefs, values, and biases; experiences of the past; dreams, hopes, fears, and expectations of the future; and immediate, short-term, and long—term wants and needs—which fill your thoughts and feelings and are the major portion of the reality to which you respond. The same is true for each person you encounter.

What is important to remember is that your perceptions and "realities" are different from those of someone else because your central nervous system selectively "filters" the information as it is received by your brain.

Consider for instance, a news item—have you ever watched the news and heard several eyewitness accounts of a plane crash? If you've had, you probably noticed that the accounts differed in subtle ways. One person starts off by describing the noise of the aircraft as it crashed. Another person talks about the sight of the plane hitting the ground and bursting into flames. Still another person describes the sick feeling that came over them when they realized the plane was going to crash.

Every minute of the day your representational systems are bombarded with an incredible amount of information. Your central nervous system selectively sifts through this information, allowing only a portion of it to reach your conscious mind. This filtering process is called deletion, distortion, and generalization. Without these filters, you would be engulfed by the incessant stream of information.

Each person has his or her own unique perception of the world. Your family, friends, coworkers, neighbors, and colleagues view the world through a different set of filters than you do. What you say, what you think, and what you do may mean something totally different to them than it does to you.

Your representational systems influence your thinking, and over the time, you gradually develop preferences in the way you use them. The three primary representational systems are visual, auditory, and kinesthetic. The olfactory (smell) and gustatory (taste) systems are usually used as triggers to the other systems.

Most people will use one system more than the other two, with the result that the preferred system is the one with which fine distinctions are made. For instance, people who are influenced more by what they see are said to be visual. Other people rely more on what they hear, and they are said to be auditory. For yet others, their favorite method of focusing is through feelings and sensations, and they are known as kinesthetic.

Those people with a preference for the visual representational system think primarily in pictures. If you asked them, "Do you know John?" they would very likely reply, "Is he the tall man with the thin moustache who drives that dark blue Mustang?" instead of mentioning his accent or how they feel about him. Their visual descriptions will be more detailed than those of an auditory or kinesthetic person.

By contrast, auditory people will tend to make finer distinctions in sound than in images or feelings. After a presentation, they will often remember the exact words that a person used, but might not be able to recall as quickly the color of the speaker's dress or how they felt during the presentation. They would be more likely to remember that John had a Southern drawl. Auditory people can be easily distracted by background noise and often prefer to work in places where they have a soothing background.

People who prefer the kinesthetic system rely heavily on their feelings of experience. They would rather "get a feel" for something than look at a picture or hear about it. They would tell you that John is thick-skinned, but also has his head on his shoulders. Kinesthetics generally make good counselors and negotiators, because they can be extremely sensitive to other people's feelings.

Although most people have a preferred representational system, it does not mean that our other senses or representational systems are dormant. Rather, we use the other senses to complement what our preferred representational system communicates to us. In this way, we get a more complete picture of what is going on around us.

When you know what a person's modality is, you will know one of the most important aspects of their personality—how they perceive the world around them. This is a major factor in communication—it is a basic way in which some people are alike and others different.

A person's preferred representational system is often expressed in their choice of words. A visual person will "see the potential" of a new strategy or idea, while an auditory person will "like the way that sounds" and a kinesthetic person will tell you, "I've got a good feeling about that." By paying close attention to your customers' words, you can determine how they structure their thoughts. You won't be able to tell what they are thinking (this is not a mind-reading course!), but you can tell "how" they are thinking.

Recognizing changes in another person's state and noticing specific conditions of body posture, breathing, vocal qualities, and movement is called calibration. A person's state is constantly changing, although sometimes the change can be as subtle as an increase in their breathing rate. At other times, the change in state is obvious—a baby who was crying suddenly has a smile on its face.

Calibration is a useful tool because it requires you to step outside yourself and direct your attention to the people around you. When you do that, you can identify consciously the physiological communication that is usually taken in and processed on an unconscious level. For instance, can you remember when you were a child and your mother would get angry with you? Sometimes she didn't even have to say anything. She would get that look in her eye, and her lips would press tightly together, as if she didn't trust herself to speak. When she put her hands on her hips and squared her shoulders, then you knew you were in real trouble.

By effectively calibrating nonverbal behavior, you can begin to understand human thinking and behavior. You can do this by directing your conscious efforts to seeing, hearing, and sensing the other person's internal representations through their external manifestation of it. What you are actually doing is noting the other person's behavioral manifestations of internal representations ("BMIRs"). This is one of the most obvious mental access points, or MAPS. For instance, if I know that you are making pictures internally (visual), then I can establish deep rapport with you by entering your world using visual language. Or, if I know that you are talking to yourself internally (auditory digital), my rapport-building behavior will involve auditory language. Conversely, if I am aware that your experience is centering on kinesthetic awareness, then my language will be oriented toward touch and feelings.

The following information covers physiological clues you can look out for to determine "how" your customer is thinking, rather than what the person is thinking.

> **Body posture**: People often assume systematic, habitual postures when deep in thought and talking. These postures can indicate a great deal about the sensory representational system the person is using. The following are some typical examples:

- **Visual**: Leaning back with head and shoulders up or rounded. Chin tends to be pointed up.
- **Auditory**: Body leaning forward, head cocked (as though listening), shoulders back, arms folded.
- **Kinesthetic**: Head and shoulders down. Body leaning slightly to the person's right.

Exercise: Identifying Body Posture Cues
Political Interview

Watching a political interview on television is an excellent chance to practice the skill of identifying body posture cues. These programs often depict real people responding to questions subconsciously (as opposed to a political debate, where the responses are often scripted). For this exercise, you will practice identifying body posture cues by watching a political interview show such as "Meet the Press" or "Politically Incorrect."

First, I recommend that you tape the show, but don't watch it while you are taping it. Then, when you are ready to begin this exercise, rewind the tape to the beginning. Now you are ready to begin the exercise. Turn off the sound so that you will be able to give your full attention to the nonverbal cues used by each person. Observe the body posture of the host and guest at the beginning of the show and describe it in the space provided below. As the show progresses, note any changes you observe in body posture. At the conclusion of the interview, look over your notes and write down what you believe is the representational system of the guest and the host based on your observations of their body posture. Then watch the interview again, this time with the sound on. Did their words confirm the representational system you selected? Why? Or why not?

Visual: Leaning back with head and shoulders up or rounded. Chin tends to be pointed up.

Auditory: Body leaning forward, head cocked (as though listening), shoulders thrown back, arms folded.

Kinesthetic: Head and shoulders down. Body leaning slightly to the person's right.

Beginning body posture, interviewer: _____

_____

_____

Beginning body posture, guest: _____

_____

_____

Changes in body posture, interviewer: _____

_____

_____

Changes in body posture, guest: _____

_____

_____

What is the interviewer's preferred representational system, based on body posture?

_____

What is the guest's preferred representational system, based on body posture?

_____

Accessing Cues: When people are thinking and speaking, they cue or trigger certain types of sensory representations in a number of different ways, including breathing rate, "grunts and groans," facial expressions, snapping their fingers, scratching their heads, and so on. Some of these are unique to the individual and need to be noticed and "calibrated" to the particular person performing the behaviors. Many of these cues, however, are associated with particular sensory processes and can be generalized across individuals. The following are some typical examples:

- **Visual:** High (in the chest), shallow breathing, eyes squinting, voice at higher pitch and faster tempo.
- **Auditory:** Diaphragmatic breathing, knitted brow, fluctuating voice tone and tempo.
- **Kinesthetic:** Deep abdominal breathing, deep breathy voice in lower tempo.

Exercise: Breathing, Tone and Tempo—Social Setting

The easiest way to master the skill of identifying breathing patterns is practice, practice, and more practice. For this exercise, you will observe the breathing, vocal tone, and tempo of people in a social setting. These may be people you have just met or people you have known a long time. As you do this, note the situation also. Can you identify their preferred representational system based on their breathing, vocal tone, and tempo?

- **Visual**: High (in the chest), shallow breathing, eyes squinting, voice at higher pitch and faster tempo.
- **Auditory**: Diaphragmatic breathing, knitted brow, fluctuating vocal tone and tempo.
- **Kinesthetic**: Deep abdominal breathing, deep breathy voice in lower tempo.

Name: _____

How long have you known this person? _____

Describe the social setting: _____

_____

_____

What is their breathing, vocal tone and tempo? _____

_____

What is their preferred representational system? _____

> **Gestures**: People will often touch, point to, or use gestures indicating the sensory organ which they are using. Some typical examples include:
>
> - **Visual**: Touching or pointing to the eyes; gestures made at or above eye level.
> - **Auditory**: Pointing toward and gesturing near the ears; touching the mouth or jaw. Stroking the chin thoughtfully.
> - **Kinesthetic**: Touching the chest and stomach area; gestures made below the neck.

Eye Movements: Automatic, unconscious eye movements usually accompany a particular thought process, indicating that the person is accessing one or more of the sensory representational systems. This theory has not been proven, and there is some debate as to its foundation, but to this author it appears to be useful in understanding the next level of communications.

When people are thinking and talking, they move their eyes in what are known as eye-scanning patterns. These movements appear to be symptomatic of their attempts to gain access to internally stored or internally generated information in their central nervous system. This information is encoded in the speaker's mind in one or more of the representational systems. When a person "goes inside" to retrieve a memory or to create a new thought, the person "makes pictures," and/or "talks to himself/herself," and/or "has feelings and kinesthetic sensations."

With a little bit of practice, eye-scanning patterns are easily observable behavior. When you see people talking and thinking, you can notice their eyes are constantly in motion, darting back and forth, up and down, occasionally glancing at objects and people, but just as often "focused" on inner experiences. As previously mentioned, these movements are symptomatic of the way they are thinking. In the descriptions that we will be discussing, "looking" refers to the movements of a person's eyes in the direction indicated. "Left" means toward the speaker's left and "right" means toward his/her right. It is helpful to keep in mind that this accessing behavior represents "looking" internally. That is, during the moment of information retrieval, people are generally not conscious of external visual stimuli. Rather, they are concentrating on internally stored or generated images, sounds, words, and feelings. Please notice also that the words in parentheses in each category indicate the kind of information being accessed.

Body Posture Exercises
Body Posture and Eye-Accessing Cues—Workplace

Combine the skills you have learned and observe the body posture and the eye-accessing cues of the people in your workplace. As you do this, note the situation also. For instance, you might observe people in the course of a company meeting, with a client, a chance meeting in the hall, etc. See if you can determine their preferred representational system based on their body posture. Then take note of their eye-movement cues. Do their eye-accessing cues indicate the same preferred representational system? Which cues are easier to identify? Why?

- **Visual Body Posture Cues:** Person leans back, with head and shoulders up or rounded. There is also a tendency to hold the chin up.
- **Eye-Accessing Cues:** Person looks up to their right or left or may stare straight ahead, eyes unfocused.
- **Auditory Body Posture Cues**: Person leans forward, with the head cocked (as though listening), shoulders back, and arms folded.
- **Eye-Accessing Cues**: Person looks sideways to the left or right, or may look down to the left (internal dialogue).
- **Kinesthetic Body Posture Cues:** Person has their head and shoulders down, with the body leaning slightly to the person's right.
- **Eye-Accessing Cues:** Person looks down and to the right.

Name: _____

Job Description:

Situation:

Body Posture Cues:

Eye-Accessing Cues:

Preferred Representational System:

Did their body posture cues and their eye-accessing cues indicate the same representational system?

Which cues were easier to identify? Why?

Representational Systems

Seeing (Visual)

- Eyes: These people look up to their right or left or their eyes may appear unfocused.
- Gestures: Their gestures are quick and angular, and include pointing.
- Breathing and speech: High, shallow, and quick.
- Words: The words that capture their attention include: *see, look, imagine, perspective, reveal.*
- Presentations: They prefer pictures, diagrams, and movies.

Hearing (Auditory)

- Eyes: These people look down to the left and may appear "shifty-eyed."
- Gestures: Their gestures are rhythmic, touching one's face (i.e., rubbing the chin).
- Breathing and speech: Midchest, rhythmic.
- Words: The words that capture their attention include: *hear, listen, ask, tell, clicks, in-tune.*
- Presentations: They prefer list, summaries, quotes, readings.

Feeling (Kinesthetic)

- Eyes: These people look down to the right.
- Gestures: Their gestures are rhythmic, touching chest.
- Breathing and speech: Deep, slow with pauses.
- Words: The words that capture their attention include: *feel, touch, grasp, catch on, contact.*
- Presentations: They prefer hands-on, do-it demonstrations, test drives.

Identifying Your Representational System

For each of the following questions, think about the person, place, or object described and circle the first answer that comes to your mind. Check your responses with the assessment key provided.

1. When you think of coffee, what comes to your mind first?

    a. An image, e.g., a cup filled to the brim with rich, dark coffee
    b. A sound, e.g., coffee dripping into the glass carafe
    c. A touch, e.g., the warmth of the cup filled with coffee
    d. A smell, e.g., the aroma of coffee as you lift the cup to your mouth
    e. A taste, e.g., the rich taste as you take your first sip

2. When you think back to what you did on your last birthday, what is the first thing you remember?

    a. A taste, e.g., something you ate
    b. A sound, e.g., a song you heard on the radio
    c. A smell, e.g., of your environment
    d. A touch, sensation or emotion
    e. An image or picture, e.g., some place that you went

3. When you think about your favorite restaurant, what do you think of first?

    a. What you see, e.g., the décor, or the people you are with
    b. An emotion or touch, e.g., how you felt when you were there
    c. Something you hear, e.g., the conversation, the music
    d. A taste, e.g., your favorite dish
    e. A smell, e.g., the aroma from the kitchen

4. When you think of your childhood and the house that you grew up in, which of these come to mind first?

    a. A smell, e.g., mom baking cookies in the kitchen
    b. A sound, e.g., conversation as the family gathered together
    c. A taste, e.g., mom's macaroni and cheese casserole
    d. An emotion or touch, e.g., a feeling of security, or the smooth wooden banister you held on to, as you came down the stairs
    e. An image, e.g., the way to the house after the first snowfall

5. When you think about something humorous, what do you first think about?

  a. An emotion, e.g., someone tickling your feet
  b. A sound, e.g., a joke you heard
  c. An image, e.g., a favorite pet playing with a toy
  d. A smell e. A taste

6. When you think about your workplace, what is the first thing that you think about?

  a. A touch or an emotion, e.g., how you feel about the work you do
  b. A sound, e.g., of machinery or other people's voices
  c. A taste
  d. A picture, e.g., what you do while at work
  e. A smell, e.g., of the environment

7. When you think about something you do that is physically challenging, what do you think about first?

  a. A sound or a conversation you have with yourself
  b. A touch or an emotion
  c. An image or a picture
  d. A taste
  e. A smell

8. When you think about your closest family member (spouse, mother, father, sister, brother), what do you think about first?

  a. An image, e.g., what they looked like the last time you saw them
  b. A smell, e.g., the favorite cologne or perfume they like to wear
  c. A sound, e.g., their voice
  d. An emotion, e.g., you feelings for them
  e. A taste, e.g., a meal you shared together

9. When you think about your favorite thing to do on the weekend, what comes to your mind first?

  a. A taste, e.g., a favorite food, like barbecued ribs
  b. A sound associated with doing this, e.g., the sharp crack of a baseball bat connecting with a ball

    c. An emotion or touch, e.g., how you feel when you think of spending your time this way

    d. A smell from the environment, e.g., the flowers at your favorite park

    e. An image, e.g., who you would do this with or where you would be

10. When you think about a major disappointment in your life (e.g., a promotion or job you didn't get or a test you failed), what do you think of first?

    a. A taste

    b. A touch, e.g., the feel of something, or emotion, e.g., what you felt when you heard the news

    c. An image or picture, e.g., where you were

    d. A sound, e.g., what you heard or what you said to yourself

    e. A smell

11. When you think about something physical that you don't like to do, e.g., taking out the garbage or weeding the garden, what comes to mind first?

    a. A touch, e.g., the feel of the weed as you pull it from the ground, or an emotion, e.g., how you feel about doing this task

    b. A taste

    c. A smell, e.g., the smell of the garbage as you carry it to the trash can

    d. An image, e.g., the weeds against the dark earth

    e. A sound, e.g., the cricket's chirping near the garden or the rustle of the garbage bag?

12. When you think about taking a vacation in the Bahamas, what do you think of first?

    a. A sound, e.g., the laughter of children as they play in the surf

    b. An image, e.g., palm trees swaying in the breeze against a brilliant blue sky

    c. A smell, e.g., the salty air from the ocean

    d. A taste, e.g., a cool, refreshing drink

    e. A touch, e.g., the feel of the warm sun as you relax on the hotel deck

	Visual	Auditory	Kinesthetic	Olfactory (Smell)	Gustatory (Taste)
1	A	B	C	D	E
2	E	B	D	C	A
3	A	C	B	E	D
4	E	B	D	A	C
5	C	B	A	D	E

6	D	B	A	E	C
7	C	A	B	E	D
8	A	C	D	B	E
9	E	B	C	D	A
10	C	D	B	E	A
11	D	E	A	C	B
12	B	A	E	C	D
Total					

Circle the letter that corresponds to your choice for each question. Add up the total number of letters circled in each column. These totals are an indication of your preferred representational system. The column with the highest score is most likely your preferred representational system.

Note: You will need to focus on the representational systems that you are the weakest in. Pick the one you used the least and for the next few days use those words as much as possible. Then go to the second weakest. This will build in added flexibility in you communication. It will also allow you to cross-reference much easier.

Each representational system has sensory-based words called predicates (verbs, adverbs, and adjectives). This is useful because sometimes your initial contact with someone will be over the phone. To determine their preferred representational system, listen to the words they select and notice which predicates are used most often. Once you become familiar with the language of the different modalities, you can then choose words that will literally "make more sense" to the people with whom you want to develop rapport.

Building Self-Confidence

This is a way to respond to criticism and stay resourceful, whether it is at home, at work, or with friends. It enables you to use criticism as feedback to improve your relationships.

1. See yourself in front of you. That self in front of you is going to learn a new approach to criticism while you watch from the outside. Do whatever you need to do to feel detached from that self. You can see that self farther away, in black-and-white, or behind Plexiglas, etc.

2. Watch and listen as that self gets criticized and instantly dissociates. There are several ways that self can dissociate. He/she can surround him/herself with a Plexiglas shield when he/she was criticized. Or that self can see the words of criticism printed within a cartoon balloon (like the comic strips), etc. That self uses one of these methods to keep feeling neutral or resourceful.

3. Watch as that self makes a slide or movie of what the criticizer is saying. What does the person mean? Does that self have enough information to make a clear, detailed picture? If the answer is "no," gather information. If the answer is "yes," proceed to the next step.

4. Have that self decide on a response. For example, that self can agree with any part of the criticism you agree with. Or that self could apologize, saying, "I'll give it some serious thought," or "I see things differently now," and so forth.

5. Does that self want the information you got from this criticism to act differently next time? If so, have that self select a new behavior. That self will then imagine using the new behavior in detail in the future. Next, that self can step into this movie of using the new behavior to feel what it will be like.

6. Having watched that self go through this entire strategy, so you want this for yourself? If the answer is "no," ask inside how you modify this strategy so it fits you. If the answer is "yes," continue.

7. Thank that self for being a special resource to you in learning this strategy. Now pull that self into you, feeling him/her fill you, so that this knowledge becomes fully integrated into you.

Story: The Eagle

I am reminded of a couple of stories about Native Americans.

In the first, a young man was talking to the Medicine Man, kind of the spiritual warrior of the Hopi tribe, the oldest tribe in the U.S. He asked the Medicine Man how he always made good decisions. The Medicine Man replied:

Like most people I seem to have two dogs in me: a White dog that wants to do good things and a Black dog that wants to do bad things.

Which one wins? The one I feed the most.

Native Americans also have a reverence for eagles. That is true across all the tribes. At one time, there were eagles all over the United States, from the Florida Keys up to Alaska. They are coming back. But of course, they called many birds "eagles."

The turkey was the earth eagle because they could use almost every part of the turkey, so they called it the Ground Eagle. It was grounded but it gave them life.

They called the owl the Night Eagle, because he could see at night. Wouldn't it be nice to see things that other people can't see?

They had several different types of eagles that represented power, grace, freedom, discipline, and integrity, because it doesn't kill maliciously and just seemed above it all.

It just kind of watches and keeps and eye on things. That is why it was a matter of pride to find and wear an eagle feather.

Most tribes shared certain things in common. When they went through changes, in life they would change their name.

You were given a birth name, but once you came of age, you picked your own name—you were your own person; you changed.

They would also change their name again when they were going through major changes in life.

If their spouse died, they change their name. If they won or lost a battle, they would change their name.

Maybe we can't change our names, but we can change the language we use with ourselves.

I had a friend who was a farmer, and one day he was walking past his chickens. He glanced at them and saw there was one that was ugly, a butt-ugly chicken. Every time he looked at it, it got bigger and uglier.

One day he noticed that it was a lot bigger than the rest. A friend of his who happened to walk by noticed the ugly chicken and said, "Hey, man! Now how did you get an eagle in there? That's not a chicken, that's an eagle!" It acted like a chicken, but was in reality an eagle.

He let this eagle, who thought he was a chicken, grow. The eagle felt rather restricted, for he was now bigger—he was overpowering. And slowly, he began to feel different than the others.

He had different drives and urges. Finally he said to one of his friends, after a mouse walked by, "Don't you ever just want to get one of those, rip one apart, and eat it?" The chickens were upset and said, "You cannibal!" He talked with one of the older chickens, and they didn't know what he should do.

The farmer took the eagle and put him up in the loft of the barn and left him there for the day. The eagle began noticing that he could really see a lot of things from up here—he saw a rabbit hopping around about a quarter mile away, birds flying, etc.

After a while he began to get hungry. Even the corn started to look good because the hungrier you get, the better things looked. He didn't know what to do. He got pretty hungry and couldn't stand it anymore. Some of our mothers used to say, if you get hungry enough, it will move you to action!

So he took a deep breath and said, "You know I am going to jump down there and eat; if the fall kills me at least, it is over. If I have to stay up here and starve to death, I may as well do something?" So he closed his eyes, took a deep breath, and I don't know if eagles have knees, but he bent his legs and he jumped!

The moment he did, nature took over and he spread his wings. And as his wings shot out . . . that six-foot wingspan . . . a breeze caught him, and he began to soar. He opened his eyes for a moment, and it scared the hell out of him. All of a sudden, he looked down and he was two hundred feet in the air, and he didn't even know how he did it.

Because he took that little act of faith of just closing his eyes and jumping, there he was, flying around, and he didn't know what to do! Then he found he could do some stuff; he flapped his wings and it made him go higher. He could tilt his wings like a jet and cut this way and cut that way. Innately, his brain and instincts took over.

He was having fun. After a while he saw a rabbit; he thought about it. He thought about the corn in the barnyard, eyed the rabbit, thought about the corn, the rabbit, the corn, dipped his wings, and ate the rabbit.

The minute he finished, he realized it was the best meal he had ever had; it was the way he was meant to eat, like a king. He felt guilty. He was trained to do what chickens normally did, not to do this.

He flew back to the barnyard; he circled around, and the other chickens ran and hid. The other chickens realized who he was and started to ignore him the way they always did. The eagle got upset and went to one of the old roosters, a kind of mentor to the chickens.

The rooster, for the first time, gave him some good advice. He said, "Maybe you are just different, not good or bad, just different.

"You look different, you act different. Sometimes it takes more courage to leave what you have always known. You know you shouldn't be here, so whatever choice you make is going to be rough."

He left and saw another large bird flying. He dipped his eagle wings and realized he can really move. The other bird was a hawk. The hawk was afraid at first because eagles eat hawks, more like they own the sky. The hawk feared the eagle at first, but the eagle just wanted to talk.

The eagle said, "I am just a big chicken flying around here."

The hawk said, "Chicken, you are an eagle. It's your sky—you can do whatever you want! It's your call!"

The eagle said, "But I live on the ground."

The hawk answered, "No, you don't. You are supposed to live in the trees and the air."

Somebody had to point it out. So the eagle left, and he landed in the trees and began to do things that came quite naturally to him. Within no time he learned to hunt, dive, and fish. One day he saw another eagle flying by, and he felt some stirrings inside. It was a girl eagle. They paired off and began to talk and she was fascinated by his background.

He took her to the barnyard. She said, "It's interesting down here! But I really don't like the smell; I don't like the people either! Other than that I guess it's all right."

He turned out to be quite an asset to the other eagles because he brought a different perspective they never had. He brought a chicken's view of the world to them. And that maybe they had a gift, that maybe they didn't even know they had up there, because he had to climb up through the ranks, so to speak.

Joe versus the Volcano

In the movie *Joe versus the Volcano*, there is a scene where they were out in the middle of the ocean, after the boat sunk, and they were out in the water by themselves. The power of the movie is the guy only had the guts to live when he knew he was going to die. That takes some courage.

If we realize that we are all mortal, we better begin to think about what is it we want to do. What is our passion, our purpose, our mission.

Like one of my idols, Jedi knight Anakin Skywalker. If you have a passion it will literally move the universe. You can shift people beyond their wildest dreams. Whether it is one person at a time, a small group at a time, a nation at a time or a Universe.

Back to the movie *Joe versus the Volcano*. It is about hope, and reaching beyond yourself. In this special scene he is out there in the ocean, and if any of you have been out on the ocean at night, when the moon comes up, it is an interesting experience. It's huge; it's gigantic. In the movie, he looks at it and remembers; he thinks he is going to die from exposure.

He is standing there, and he looks up to the moon and says, "God, whom I do not understand, thank you for my life."

And what I ask is:

If you can have just a little bit of that kind of gratitude for some of the talents, tools, and abilities you have been given—and you all have these different talents, tools, and abilities . . . you can really move the world. But sometimes it is hard to take that in and have the gratitude in your attitude so to speak. Just to be thankful for your life.

Mind control is perhaps one of the least explored sciences in the world. Many think that it is just not possible. But we are here to prove that it is indeed very possible.

You do not have to be a wizard or a sorcerer; all you need to do is read this book till you have mastered all the techniques described. After all, it's not very difficult, is it? So here's wishing you all success as you go around exercising your power over others.

So I'm not sure, now that you are ready to start testing your skill, if you have ever felt like it was time to close your eyes and take that leap. It can be a very scary thing. But I encourage you to spread your wings and sometimes just take that leap of faith. It is just the hardest thing we ever have to do. It can be overwhelming. But usually nature takes over and takes care of itself.

CHAPTER 10

The Fourth Key
Turning Your Fear into Power and
Controlling Your Internal State

It is now time to begin to take your skills to the real world. I want you to use and master this technology, and for this you need to be able to control your own internal state. After teaching this for years, I see how students want to use this, but a fear overtakes them and they clam up. It is against this background that I would like to introduce a technique that will have you go out there and use your skills.

You are a student of mind control. You're out and you see someone you want to meet. You review the rapport skills in your head, you are ready to approach your target, your stomach tightens, you get feelings you tell yourself you should not have, like doubt and fear. It sort of feels like you're a kid again! Do people read this inaction as your fear state? The fear overcomes you. Your heart races and you have difficulty catching your breath. Your hands tremble, your vision blurs, your hearing shuts off, and your mind fills with negative thoughts. You "naturally" interpret these sensations as fear. Then, because of your studying mind control techniques, you feel guilty, and then you begin to doubt yourself.

The same thing happens when you start to approach your boss about a raise—you have the skills and know your rapport skills are there, but you freeze.

Where is the Zen-like peace of a mind control master? Where are the techniques you've worked on? You ask yourself, why am I afraid? The other person looks calm. You pray your skills will kick in, but will they?

Mind Training 101

To do this, you must first be able to understand the difference between an "adrenal push" and its physical effects, and the psychological state we label as fear, and make friends with both. They will happen, and we can put them to good use.

Let's look at the psychobiological stages of this state we call fear. To do this, we must separate the physical responses from the psychological interpretations of them. This is the first step to overcoming them.

Fear is defined as a strong, often unpleasant, emotional and physical response to real or PERCEIVED danger.

Physical

Adrenaline is a natural hormone secreted by the adrenal glands—this is nature's response to stressful environmental triggers. Its only job is to prepare the body for action, fight or flight. It ought to be your ally. It comes in basically four steps:

Preevent. There is a slow release of adrenaline. This state occurs often. Many people refer to it as a stress reaction. You're tense, slightly nervous, and on edge. If this state is prolonged, it can exhaust you. (This is why high stress jobs "burn" you out.) This state is intended to put you on alert, both physically and mentally. It also releases neurotransmitters for heightened mental focus. Fear of fear can increase this.

Event Rush or Adrenal Dump. This occurs rapidly and very intensely. It is when your adrenal glands "dump" large amounts of the hormone into your system. This is to prepare you for major physical activity. Fight or flight. The effects of adrenaline are varied, but it is important to remember that this state is the ultimate survival tool. Adrenaline can cause:

- Tightening of the muscles in preparation for trauma.
- Visual exclusion. Narrowing of vision. This causes you to lose your peripheral vision, creating tunnel vision.
- Auditory exclusion. You lose a high percentage of your hearing. (It's why you can't hear the crowd noise during an athletic event.)
- Speeded up heart rate.
- Release of ATP to give extra physical strength, but it causes rapid exhaustion. (It gives you the shakes!)
- Rapid cognitive activity. You get a load of thoughts flooding your mind, usually negative; can make you feel overwhelmed.
- Increase in breathing.

Remember, none of these things, in and of themselves, is bad and is therefore not to be feared. They prepare your body for action. People who channel this into productive use excel in tense/stressful situations. These are the people who do better on rank tests and other events when most people go down a notch.

In-Event Adrenaline. This is a second dump that increases the effects of the above as well as:

- Blocks pain
- Gives a secondary rush of energy
- Creates extra negative thoughts—fighting doubts

This state is intended to give you that "second wind," extra physical endurance, strength and power to finish an "event" (fight-flight, etc.). This state explains why some people get better as a game (or fight) goes on. This is why in football, some athletes go out of their way to hit or get hit a few times, to get into the flow of the game.

Postevent Adrenaline Drip. After an event, the adrenal glands secrete small amounts of adrenaline. This causes slightly higher physical tension and leads to mentally repeating the event—reliving the fight. This state is much like the first and is intended to help your body readjust to the effects of the stressful event. This leads to physical and mental exhaustion.

Now that you can understand that the physical states are intended to help you, you can see the importance of not labeling these as good or bad. Just accept that these states are and then let the mind take over and channel this extra energy from adrenaline to good use. Insight and knowledge are only the first steps.

How to Channel Fear into Power

To learn to harness this process, the first step is to recognize that it is normal. Insight and knowledge to this opens the door, and now we can learn to channel this wonderful, power-packed state to give you an edge in hostile situations.

The first step is to find and identify the first feelings of "fear"—the preevent adrenaline release:

- How do you feel?
- Where do you feel it (Stomach, chest, shoulders, back, etc.)?
- How is your state of mind?

To do this exercise, think of something that makes you fearful (confrontation with your boss, IRS audit, approaching that special someone, etc.). Really relive it and notice the above sensations. Now label it and store this information.

Develop a "Circle of Power or Excellence"

Think of a time you were at your very best. You were in control. You were physically and mentally sharp. It could be a class you did well at, or a sporting event, or a business deal. You were focused and sharp. Now imagine a circle on the floor—and it is your "Circle of Excellence and Power."

- What color is it?
- Does it have a sound?
- What else do you notice?

Think of the event from above and step into your "Circle." Breathe in deeply. Breathe the "Circle" into you. Throw your shoulders back. Feel the focus and power. Repeat this twice.

Step out of the "Circle" and reaccess the fearful state. As you begin to feel the fear (adrenaline state), step into the circle and breathe in. Do this five times.

This is true Fear into Power!

Search in vain for that old fearful state. As you start to access fear, you will naturally go into a state of power.

Now that we have a basis for blocking the old fear response, you can take it to the next level to excel. Once you are able to convert fear into power, you can face, as Tsunetomo Yamamoto, an eighteenth-century samurai, once said in his famous writing "Hagakure" (which translates to hidden among the leaves): "The realization of certain death should be renewed every morning.

"Each morning you must prepare yourself for every kind of death with composure of mind. Imagine yourself broken by bows, guns, spears, swords, carried off by floods, leaping into a huge fire, struck by lightning, torn apart by earthquake, plunging from a cliff, as a disease-ridden corpse."

It may sound morbid, but if you imagine your deepest fears, death, humiliation, loss of pride, etc. and step into power, you will be in a better position to face whatever comes your way. It will start to develop the heart of a warrior. You will be the type of person who is a master of their own mind, which is the basis for mastering others.

People follow others who are confident and show little fear. This is what we want in our leaders. Take this attitude and feeling with you into the rest of this book. WELCOME TO THE WORLD FEW HAVE BEEN EXPOSED TO, that is, TRUE MIND CONTROL.

TWENTY-ONE-DAY EXERCISE

Day 1: Sensor Acuity

- Take a different view of the world.
- Notice coworkers' or friends' hair, the color, the style.
- Notice the color and texture of the walls of your workspace.
- Sit in a different spot when you eat a meal.
- Notice the color of all your family/coworkers' eyes.
- Wear your watch (or other jewelry) on a different hand.

Day 2: Rapport

- Mirror/match the physiology of three people, coworker, friend/family member, stranger in a social setting.
- Be obvious.

Day 3: Anchoring

- Notice several self-anchoring experiences
- Auditory: music—what songs motivate you? Get you going? Calm you down?
- Visual: find visual anchors that affect you—dogs, babies, the flag.
- Olfactory/Gustatory: walk into a bakery or other similar establishment; close your eyes, and what do you notice?

Day 4: Review Basic NLP Techniques

- Which is your favorite and what specifically about it causes you to choose it?
- Do this to someone in a casual interaction.

Day 5: State Control

- Maintain a high state (motivation, excitement, focus) for as long as possible.
- What do you have to do to reenter it?

Day 6: Meta Model

- Do the short version of the meta model; gather information from a coworker or acquaintance.
- No advice! Gather info!

Day 7: Presuppositions

- Notice the response to your communication; is it the response you want?
- If not, what can you do differently?
- The meaning of the communication is the response to elicit!

Day 8: Acuity

- Put on your clothes in another way.
- Drink your coffee, soda, etc. with the opposite hand.
- Open up your vision by noticing the details in things you do daily.

Day 9: Rapport

- Go to restaurant and mirror the waiter/waitress. Then match their language and breathing.
- Can you notice their state?
- Can you change it?

Day 10: Anchoring

- Get a coworker or friend to laugh. As they do, anchor this.
- Try a few times.
- Can you elicit the response with your anchor?

Day 11: State

- Notice an unresourceful state in yourself. Can you notice the stimulus?
- Change your state and keep it changed.

Day 12: Meta Model

- Can you notice how many times people delete/distort/generalize in a conversation?
- Try to recover a small amount of this lost info by asking: specifically?

Day 13: Techniques

- Do the swish pattern on yourself, then on someone else.

Day 14: Presuppositions

- Flexible—take an approach to something that will surprise your friends or coworkers.
- Come up with a different way to solve a common problem.
- "The person with the most flexibility will control or influence a situation."

Day 15: Acuity

- Watch people interact in a public setting.
- Mirror/match them. Can you understand the communication?
- Can you "sense" their emotions?

Day 16: Rapport

- Go to a store or car dealer.
- You get into rapport with the salesperson.
- See if you can influence them to give you some "inside" information.

Day 17: Anchoring

- Watch commercials and see how many "anchors" you notice, i.e., oldies music to set the mood, use of flag.
- Now that you recognize the anchors, does it de-anchor you?

Day 18: State

- Elicit a strong state in someone by you entering into it, and then change your state quickly.
- What happens?

Day 19: Meta Model

- Listen to a conversation in a public place.
- After noticing meta model violations, what are their basic representational systems?

Day 20: Techniques

- Do the new behavior generator and/or chaining anchors on a coworker.

Day 21: Presuppositions

- Notice how many times someone mistakes the map for the territory—their way is the only way.
- "The map is not the territory."

Bonus:

1. Pick your weakest representational system VAR and use it all day like it is a favorite.
2. Pick a technique you rarely do (or dislike) and find persons to do it.
3. Try to take another's position in a conversation—step into their shoes.
4. Break down one of your normal tasks into small chunks. Can you improve it?

Repeat Days 1-21. You're a master in training!

Putting It Together— Einstein's Brain

In the June 19, 1999 issue of *Lancet* (the journal of the British Medical Association), Sandra F. Witelson, Ph.D., Debra L. Kigar, and Thomas Harvey, M.D., of the Department of Psychiatry and Behavioral Neurosciences of McMaster University in Canada have reported that the differences in the brain of Albert Einstein may explain his genius in mathematics. When the Nobel Prize-winning physicist died of a ruptured abdominal aorta in 1955 at the age of seventy-six, his brain was removed and preserved within seven hours of his death. His medical history was well documented, and biographies show he was mentally adept, doing research until the end of his life. There had never been a report describing the anatomy of his brain until now.

In the McMaster University study, the researchers compared anatomical measurements from Einstein's brain with the brains from thirty-five men and fifty-six women who had normal intelligence. These researchers also studied the brains of eight men over sixty-five so they could take into account changes that normally occur with aging.

Einstein's brain appeared similar to the others except for two areas found on each side of the brain called the inferior parietal regions. Einstein had extensive development in these regions on both sides of his brain; his brain was almost 15 percent wider than the control group.

It is thought that the growth of this region seems to have occurred early in the development of his brain, because it appears to have blocked the development of a groove in the brain called the Slyvian fissure. In most people, the Slyvian fissure runs along each side of the brain reaching about three-quarters of the way to the back. In Dr. Einstein's case, the fissure does not reach as far back as normal, but instead it turns upward to join another groove that normally runs down the side of the brain called the postcentral sulcus.

The confluence of these, the Slyvian fissure and the postcentral sulcus, forms a C-shaped groove on the surface of each side of his brain. "This morphology found in each of Einstein's hemispheres was not seen in any hemispheres of the 35 control male brains or of any of the 56 female brains, nor in any specimen documented in the published collections of post-mortem brains," write Dr. Witelson and her colleagues.

The area of Einstein's brain that appears to be overdeveloped is thought to be involved in the creation and manipulation of three-dimensional spatial images and the mathematical representation of those concepts, the researchers write.

Therefore, the unusual anatomy of Einstein's brain may explain why he tended to think about scientific problems visually. "Einstein's own description of his scientific thinking," the researchers write, "was that words do not seem to play any role, but there is associative play of more or less clear images of a visual and muscular type."

There were other differences that might explain Einstein's abilities. Because of the differences in the grooves along the side of his brain, the neurons (cells) of a particular area of the parietal operculum are not divided by one of the grooves, but are instead kept together. The researchers speculate that the absence of this groove may have allowed more neurons in this area to establish better connections between each other. They further think that this may have created an "extraordinarily large expanse of highly integrated cortical network."

It is thought that when large, well-integrated networks form in an area dedicated to certain mental tasks, it may make the person much better than normal at doing those tasks. In Einstein's case it was visualizing solutions to difficult mathematical problems. (Could this be a key to why some people have difficulty in visualizing?)

"Einstein's exceptional intellect in these cognitive domains and his self-described mode of scientific thinking may be related to the atypical anatomy in his brain," the researchers concluded.

Remote Brain Control

John Chapin of the Hahnemann School of Medicine reports in *Nature Neuroscience* that they have trained six lab rats to move a robot arm with the power of thought alone. First the rats were trained in the classical S-R way to press a spring-loaded lever (which moves a robotic arm) using their paws to get a reward (water or food). This allowed the researchers to ascertain which brain cells were involved in the task. Thus, having their target cell-groups (parts of the brain in the motor cortex and the thalamus) the researchers implanted arrays of electrodes into these groups to study the role of individual neurons in them. They now had a detailed outline on the neuronal activity that gives rise to the bending, pushing, and stretching movements that constitute pressing a lever.

Through analysis, over many hundreds of trials of the firing patterns that make up such a movement, the researchers located the neurons responsible for every stage of the action: preparation, flexing the forelimb, extending it, pushing it, and so on. Then the team harnessed these neurons for their own by wiring them so that they could fire them directly and move the arm without the animal touching the lever. With this new setup, the rats quickly learned that there was no need to physically push the lever in order for a reward. A few tries later, they were able to reconfigure their brain activity so that it alone moved the reward-bearing robotic arm.

This is the first time that brain activity, so high up in the motor pathways, has been used to drive a machine. Older devices used cruder signals from the stumps of amputated limbs or the surface of the skin. This new technology will offer far greater speed and precision.

When you look at these two diverse studies, I am drawn to the hypothesis that if rats can learn to control brain activity, can we, as a somewhat higher developed animal, use our conscious thought to direct energy to the parts of our brains that do different tasks? And could we stimulate growth and change in the actual structure of the brain itself? There are studies that show that with conscious attention, you can cause physical changes. This is the basis of biofeedback. There is some research using MRIs to map brain activity, and again it seems to be able to be controlled by conscious attention. Once we become aware of how to do it, it seems just so possible!

We therapists who use altered states to effect mind/body changes could use our skills to do the same things. This could be our next big breakthrough, using conscious and subconscious thought to alter our physical brains, to improve them with mental exercises (hypnosis and NLP) the way athletes use physical exercise to alter their bodies. Is not your brain a physical organ capable of change and growth much like a muscle?

Try to develop ways to use your skills to bring advances in this exciting field, and let me know how it works. In my programs, such as Designing Your Destiny, second edition, tape series, much of this type of work is done.

Until next time, use the Force to spur growth in your own developing brain.

References

Witelson, S. F., Kigar, D., Harvey, T., "The Exceptional Brain of Albert Einstein," *Lancet*, 1999, vol. 353, 2149-53 19 June 1999

Deary, I. J., Carl, P. G., "Neuroscience and Human intelligence differences," *Trends Neuroscience*, 1999, no. 20 365-371

Chapin, J., *Nature Neuroscience*, June 1999

From The FBI Bulletin, reprinted with permission. Reprinting does not imply approval or endorsement of any person or product, for informational purposes only.

Subtle Skills for Building Rapport

Using Neuro-Linguistic Programming in the Interview Room

By VINCENT A. SANDOVAL, M.A., and SUSAN H. ADAMS, M.A.

*M*ark *Hamilton, a seasoned detective, slowly opens the door to the interview room. The witness to the drive-by shooting sits leaning forward in a chair with her head in her hands. Normally, Mark bellows out his introduction to establish immediate control, but not this time. He enters the room without speaking, pulls a chair close to the witness, leans forward, and, in a barely audible voice, slowly begins, "I'm Detective Mark Hamilton . . ."*

Detective Hamilton is using techniques from NeuroLinguistic Programming, a communication model with a name he might not even recognize. Yet, his years of interviewing have taught him the techniques. To establish rapport with this witness, Detective Hamilton knows that he needs to match her nonverbal behavior, or kinesics, by sitting down and leaning forward. When the witness begins to talk, Detective Hamilton listens carefully to her words and intentionally uses similar language. He also pays close attention to *how* she talks and matches her paralanguage (speech rate, volume, and pitch). In so doing, Detective Hamilton builds rapport with the witness and, hence, increases his chances of gathering pertinent information during the interview.

Detective Hamilton and other experienced investigators recognize the crucial role that rapport plays in an interview. Derived from the French verb *rapporter* meaning "to bring back," the English word *rapport* refers to a relationship or communication characterized by harmony.[1] With this in mind, the need for rapport applies to all interviews, but especially to those involving a victim or witness who has experienced physical or psychological abuse. The interviewer's task is similar to that of the clinical psychologist, who must initially develop a personal bond with his client before intimate feelings are shared.[2] Thus, investigators can enhance their rapport-building skills by examining some practical recommendations derived from the behavior modification technique known as *Neuro-Linguistic Programming.*

UNDERSTANDING NEURO-LINGUISTIC PROGRAMMING

In the early 1970s, John Grinder, an assistant professor of linguistics at the University of California in Santa Cruz, and Richard Bandler, a student of psychology, identified patterns used by successful therapists. They packaged them in a way that could be passed on to others through a model now known as Neuro-Linguistic Programming, or NLP.[3]

Neuro-Linguistic Programming embraces three simple concepts. First, the *neuro* part of NLP recognizes the fundamental idea that all human behavior originates from neurological processes, which include seeing, hearing, smelling, tasting, and feeling. In essence, people experience the world through their senses. Second, they communicate their experiences verbally, through language;[4] therefore, the *linguistic* part of NLP refers to this use of language to communicate thoughts. Finally, the *programming* aspect of NLP recognizes that individuals choose to organize their ideas and actions to produce results. Each person also decides how to organize these ideas in a specific manner.[5]

The NLP founders theorize that people think differently and that these differences correspond to individual programming or processing systems. People use their senses outwardly to perceive the world and inwardly to "re-present" this experience to themselves. In NLP, representational systems denote ways people take in, store, and code information in their minds.[6] These systems pertain to the principal human senses—seeing (visual), hearing (auditory), and feeling (kinesthetic). To a lesser degree, they involve tasting (gustatory) and smelling (olfactory). People constantly see, hear, and feel whatever transpires around them. When individuals relate these experiences to others, they mentally access the sights, sounds, or feelings associated with these experiences and communicate them through their predominant representational system.[7]

BUILDING RAPPORT WITH NLP

Enhancing communication and, hence, building rapport represents the most applicable aspect of NLP to investigators. The ability to communicate effectively and build rapport stands as one of the major contributors to a police officer's success in dealing with the public.[8] In an interview setting, effective communication involves the interviewer's skill in establishing rapport through specific actions and words, thereby building trust and encouraging the interviewee to provide information.

Others besides successful law enforcement interviewers have found NLP techniques helpful in rapport building. For example, some medical hypnotists use the concept of "matching" with highly resistant clients.[9] By simply conforming their nonverbal behavior to that of each client, by using language from the client's preferred representational system (visual, auditory, or kinesthetic), and by matching the client's volume, tone, and rate of speech (paralanguage), they often can overcome the client's reluctance to communicate.

When interviewers intentionally align themselves with a witness or suspect through these matching or mirroring techniques, the interviewee is more inclined to respond to the interviewer and subsequently provide information. As one researcher points out, "people like people who are like themselves."[10] Once interviewers establish rapport, barriers disappear, trust grows, and an exchange of information follows. To achieve these results, interviewers should match or "mirror" the interviewee's kinesics, language, and paralanguage.

Building Rapport by Matching Kinesics

Matching another person's body language or kinesics probably is the easiest and most obvious technique. Kinesic behavior typically includes gestures, posture, and movements of the body, such as the hands, arms, feet, and legs.[11] However, a difference exists between mimicry and matching. Interviewers should match another person's body language with subtlety and caution; otherwise, the person easily could become offended. People who have developed rapport tend to match each other in posture and gestures. For example, individuals conversing together often adopt the same posture. Like partners in a dance, they respond and mirror each other's movements with movements of their own, engaging in mutual responsive actions.[12]

Detective Hamilton employs the kinesics aspect of NLP in his interview. When he enters the interview room, he immediately notices the witness' posture and the position of her hands. He notes that she is leaning forward with her head down. Her posture and the position of her head speak volumes.

"Once interviewers establish rapport, barriers disappear, trust grows, and an exchange of information follows."

As Detective Hamilton introduces himself, he pulls his chair close to the witness and, just like her, leans forward in his chair with his hands in front of him. As the witness begins to open up and speak about what she has seen, her non-verbal behavior gradually follows suit, as she opens herself up by sitting back. Eventually, as her trust in Detective Hamilton grows, she feels comfortable enough to relax. She realigns her posture by sitting up and facing Detective Hamilton. Through each succeeding change in her body language, Detective Hamilton matches her behavior, thereby lending credence to the belief that the deeper the rapport has been built between two people, the closer the matching of body language.

Building Rapport by Matching Language

Because people use language to communicate thoughts, the words they choose reflect the way they think. When relating experiences, an individual uses the visual, auditory, or kinesthetic representational system to identify these experiences and communicate them to others. For example, a person whose predominant representational system is visual will say phrases, such as "I see what you mean," "that looks good to me," "we see eye to eye," or "I get the picture." On the other hand, a person whose preference is auditory will use language, such as "something tells me . . . ," "that rings a bell," "we're on the same wave length," or "that sounds okay to me." Finally, a person who is kinesthetic or "feeling" oriented will make statements, such as "I'll get in touch with you," "how does that grab you?," "you don't have to get pushy," or "how do you think I feel?"[13]

Successful investigators listen closely to the choice of words witnesses and suspects use. Then, they conform their language to match the interviewee, using similar visual, auditory, or kinesthetic phrases.

When Detective Hamilton's drive-by shooting witness finally begins to talk, she describes her situation with phrases, such as "tremendous pressure," "I feel like I'm going to pieces," and "I can't come to grips with what's happening." The detective responds to the witness' account by matching her words. When she speaks of the "tremendous pressure," he explains ways to relieve the "pressure." He continues to use kinesthetic phrases, such as "take this load off your shoulders," to communicate in her preferred representational system.

Because individuals process information in different ways, through distinct representational systems, the investigator often acquires valuable insight into the interviewee's personal preference by paying close attention to the interviewee's eye movements. According to NLP, eye movements, referred to as "eye-accessing cues,"[14] reflect the manner in which an individual processes data. Therefore, the eyes move in specified directions, depending upon the person's preferred mode of thinking. The founders of NLP concluded that eye movements reflect whether the person has a visual preference (thinks in terms of pictures), an auditory preference ("hears" sounds), or a kinesthetic preference (feels or experiences emotion) to process information.[15]

Typically, individuals move their eyes up at an angle as they remember a picture. Some people look directly to the side, which indicates that they are using the auditory mode to recall something that they probably heard before. Finally, individuals who look down at an angle appeal to kinesthetic sensations as they recollect what they felt or experienced.[16]

If an investigator observes that a witness consistently looks up at an angle, particularly when responding to questions that require recall, the interviewer can conclude, with a measurable degree of confidence, that the person is "seeing" a picture while remembering information. In NLP terms, this individual's preferred representational system is visual. The investigator can facilitate the witness' recollection of events by encouraging this visual recall through such phrases as "how did it look to you?" or "show me what you mean." If the witness looks to the side when asked a question concerning what the person saw, the investigator can encourage the witness to remember by using questions designed to stimulate auditory recall, such as "tell me what you heard" or "how did it sound to you?" Finally, if the witness looks down at an angle when asked a question by the investigator, this could indicate that the person has a kinesthetic preference. Therefore, the investigator can choose phrases that underscore the witness' feelings or emotions, such as "how did all of this feel to you?" or "can you get a handle on what took place?" By closely monitoring the movements of a person's eyes and aligning questions in accordance with the interviewee's observed preferences, investigators can build rapport, thereby enhancing communication between themselves and the people they interview. While NLP practitioners cite a direct neurological connection between eye movements and representational systems,[17] other researchers recognize the need for additional empirical studies.[18] Currently, investigators use interviewees' eye movements as another possible indicator of their preferred manner of communicating.

> "NLP is the greatest breakthrough in human communication in 100 years!" Science Digest

Building Rapport by Matching Paralanguage

Matching another person's speech patterns, or paralanguage, constitutes the final, and perhaps most effective, way to establish rapport. Paralanguage involves how a person says something or the rate, volume, and pitch of a person's speech. One researcher goes so far as to say that matching the other person's voice tone or tempo is the best way to establish rapport in the business world.[19] What may hold true in the business realm applies in the interview setting as well. Individuals can speak fast or slow, with or without pauses. They can talk in a loud or soft volume and in a high or low pitch. However, most people are unaware of their own speech rate or vocal tones. In fact, investigators do not have to match a person's voice exactly, just close enough to encourage that individual to feel understood.[20]

In the interview setting, slowing the rate of speech to correspond with the pace of a halting witness allows for recall and communication at that person's pace. By the same token, if a witness speaks with more volume and at a quick rate, the investigator should try to match the person's animated and expressive manner of speech. By listening carefully and paying close attention to *how* people speak, investigators can, in NLP terms, get "in sync" with people by matching their paralanguage.

Experienced investigators continually employ this technique, usually without even thinking about the mechanics or the process involved. Detective Hamilton also uses this aspect of NLP in his interview.

The drive-by shooting witness speaks slowly, as if searching for the right words. Detective Hamilton slows the rate of his speech, giving ample time for the witness to get her point across without feeling rushed. He lowers his voice to match her soft volume and refrains from the urge to interrupt her. As the witness becomes more excitable, speeding up her speech rate and increasing her volume, Detective Hamilton increases his rate and volume as he attempts to mirror her. In so doing, he demonstrates to the witness that he is interested in her as an individual, and this allows her to communicate what she experienced in a way that is comfortable for her.

CONCLUSION

Detective Mark Hamilton's witness begins to feel support and understanding from the interviewer, who continues to match her kinesics, language, and paralanguage. When he sees her consistently looking down to her right, he realizes that she may be processing information on the kinesthetic level and encourages her to talk about her feelings. Slowly, she begins to trust Detective Hamilton.

Unbeknown to the witness, Detective Hamilton had been matching her in specified ways until she finally felt secure enough to provide full details of the drive-by shooter and his vehicle. As a result, the witness' emotional need was met and, from Detective Hamilton's perspective, the interview was a success.

Successful investigators listen "closely to the choice of words witnesses and suspects use."

This scenario illustrates the importance of carefully observing how witnesses and suspects communicate through nonverbal, verbal, and vocal means. Neuro-Linguistic Programming is not a new concept nor used rarely. In fact, most successful interviewers employ some variation of it to gain rapport. However, by being conscious of the process and the benefits associated with NLP, interviewers can use these techniques to their advantage. By matching interviewees' nonverbal behavior, the manner in which they say something, and even their choice of words, interviewers can increase rapport and enhance communication. As a result, the potential for gaining crucial information needed to help resolve investigations improves significantly.

Endnotes

[1]   Genie Z. Laborde, *Influencing with Integrity* (Palo Alto, CA: Syntony Publishing, 1987), 27.

[2]   Ronald P. Fisher and Edward R. Geiselman, *Memory-Enhancing Techniques for Investigative Interviewing*, (Springfield, IL: Charles C. Thomas Publisher, 1992), 22.

[3] John O'Connor and John Seymour, *Introducing Neuro-Linguistic Programming* (London, England: Harper Collins Publishers, 1990), 2.

[4] Ibid., 3.

[5] Ibid., 3.

[6] Ibid., 26.

[7] Richard Bandler and John Grinder, *Frogs into Princes* (Moab, UT: Real People Press, 1979), 5.

[8] P. B. Kincade, "Are You Both Talking the Same Language?" *Journal of California Law Enforcement* 20: 81.

[9] Ibid., 19.

[10] Jerry Richardson, *The Magic of Rapport, How You Can Gain Personal Power in Any Situation* (Cupertine, CA: Meta Publications, 1987), 21.

[11] Judith A. Hall and Mark L. Knapp, *Nonverbal Communication in Human Interaction* (Fort Worth, TX: Harcourt Brace Jovanovich College Publishers, 1992), 14.

[12] Supra note 3, 19.

[13] Supra note 7, 83.

[14] Supra note 7, 35.

[15] Supra note 7, 25.

[16] Supra note 7, 25.

[17] Supra note 7.

[18] Aldert Vrij and Shara K. Lochun, "Neuro-Linguistic Programming and the Police: Worthwhile or Not?" *Journal of Police and Criminal Psychology* 12, no. 1 (1997).

[19] Supra note 1, 30.

[20] Supra note 1, 31.

MK ULTRA

From the Internet, for informational purposes only.

"The control over a person's behavior ostensibly achieved in hypnosis obviously nominates it for use in the difficult process of interrogation." So begins a CIA study of "Hypnosis in Interrogation" which appeared in the agency's classified journal Studies in Intelligence. Could placing interrogatees under trance help loosen their lips? That was one of many operational uses of hypnosis that the CIA pondered and tested.

The Studies in Intelligence article, which was written in 1960 by Edward F. Deshere, sheds some light on the CIA's interest in hypnosis, but it tells only a tiny, incomplete part of the story. Given the potential power of hypnosis to unlock the secrets of the mind, Deshere found it "surprising that nobody . . . seems to have used it in this way." He searched the literature and consulted top experts, but found no intelligence agency that "admits to familiarity with applications of the process [of hypnosis] to interrogation."

In fact, such applications had already been tested by the CIA and others, but it appears that Deshere—like most CIA officers at the time—was not privy to information about MKULTRA, the agency's super-secret program of mind and behavior control research. The program, launched in 1953 to expand on previous CIA investigations of related topics, would last until 1963.

In the mid-1970s, congressional committees investigating MKULTRA discovered that the CIA had become involved with a startling array of brainwashing techniques. The methods studied under MKULTRA included electroshock, subliminal communication, sensory deprivation and stimulation, the use of drugs (from "truth serum" to hard narcotics to LSD), and yes, even hypnosis. Many of these experiments were conducted on unwitting human subjects, and several MKULTRA projects are listed among the most appalling CIA abuses on record. (See Dossier's documented feature on MKULTRA for more information.)

Hypnosis, in fact, had attracted the interest of military and intelligence agencies years before MKULTRA. In The Search for the "Manchurian Candidate," a thorough history of the CIA's mind control work, author John Marks devoted an entire chapter to the study and use hypnosis. "No mind-control technique has more captured popular imagination—and kindled fears—than hypnosis," Marks noted. For the CIA officials tasked with turning mental abilities (and vulnerabilities) into Cold War weapons, "hypnosis offered too much promise not to be pursued."

The CIA's first major involvement with hypnosis originated in the Office of Security, which in 1950 formed special interrogation squads—each of which was staffed with an expert hypnotist—for the purpose of evaluating potential foreign agents and defectors from enemy countries. Code-named BLUEBIRD, the program was put under the command of Morse Allen, a former officer of both Naval Intelligence and the State Department, who developed an avid interest in hypnosis when he joined the CIA's Office of Security. (Shortly thereafter, BLUEBIRD took on the new codename ARTICHOKE, the project that directly preceded MKULTRA.)

According to Marks, not only did Allen consult with and employ some of the top academic experts on hypnosis, he also conducted his own experiments:

"He asked young CIA secretaries to stay after work and ran them through the hypnotic paces—proving to his own satisfaction that he could make them do whatever he wanted. He had secretaries steal SECRET files and pass them on to total strangers, thus violating the most basic CIA security rules. He got them to steal from each other and start fires. He made one of them report to the bedroom of a strange man and then go into a deep sleep."

Allen recorded the observation that "this activity clearly indicates that individuals under hypnosis might be compromised and blackmailed." Those were helpful abilities for a spy agency, to be sure, but Allen later envisioned a more extreme use of hypnosis. In 1954 he hypnotized another secretary, and convinced her while in the trance to pick up and shoot an (unloaded) gun at another secretary.

The implications were serious: agents could conceivably be induced to assassinate a target without knowing what they were doing. However, Allen had learned enough about hypnosis to be skeptical that such an operation could actually be pulled off. No one could be sure that such experimental successes could be carried over into the operational realm. Hypnosis was surely attractive, but it was also unreliable; there were simply too many variables in how subjects might act under hypnosis or under the power of post-hypnotic suggestion.

One CIA psychologist who was heavily involved in later hypnosis research, John Gittinger, saw promise but pratfalls with the technique. "Predictable absolute control is not possible on a particular individual," he concluded, and absolute control, after all, was the objective. The pre-programmed assassin remained an elusive goal.

Still, the CIA would do everything in its power to identify intelligence uses of hypnosis. In 1977, the agency informed Congress that of the 149 subprojects that were launched under MKULTRA, eight dealt with hypnosis—including two that studied "hypnosis and drugs in combination." Hypnosis research was conducted by several renowned scientists whose funding would later be traced to the CIA. At major universities and top research institutes, as well as military bases and prisons, subjects were put into trance in experiments that were intended first and foremost to advance the CIA's ability to operationalize hypnosis. (To see a declassified document on MKULTRA hypnosis experiments, click here.)

In 1960, the CIA's counterintelligence (CI) staff became involved in the effort. Intent on discovering and improving on the Soviet Union's mind games, the CI officers saw hypnosis as a "potential breakthrough in clandestine technology," as it was described in one CIA document.

For the CI staff, interest in hypnotism went beyond the theoretical into the operational. In July 1963, the CIA issued a 128-page "Counterintelligence Interrogation" manual, a document that was not made public until 1997. Among the tactics described for "coercive" interrogation of "resistant sources" was hypnosis. (ParaScope has made available both an online and a print version of this startling document.)

"The problem of overcoming the resistance of an uncooperative interrogatee is essentially a problem of inducing regression to a level at which the resistance can no longer be sustained," the

manual said. "Hypnosis is one way of regressing people."
The manual cited the work of Martin Orne, a famous psychologist
who received several CIA subsidies under MKULTRA for his
research on hypnosis and interrogation. Like other experts, Orne
concluded that hypnosis would probably be of marginal use for
this purpose. To the CI staff, Orne's generally skeptical view of the
technique was "somewhat too cautious or pessimistic."
The manual suggested, for example, that a CIA interrogator "could
tell a suspect double agent in trance that the KGB is conducting
the questioning, and thus invert the whole frame of reference" for
the interrogatee. "[O]nce the subject is tricked into believing that
he is talking to friend rather than foe, or that divulging the truth is
the best way to suit his own purposes, his resistance will be
replaced with cooperation. The value of hypnotic trance is not that
it permits the interrogator to impose his will but rather that it can
be used to convince the interrogatee that there is not valid reason
not to be forthcoming."
The manual added that hypnosis "offers one advantage not
inherent in other interrogation techniques or aides: the posthypnotic
suggestion." In certain cases, the manual instructed:
"[I]t should be possible to administer a silent drug to a resistant
source, persuade him as the drug takes effect that he is slipping
into a hypnotic trance, place him under actual hypnosis as
consciousness is returning, shift his frame of reference so that his
reasons for resistance become reasons for cooperation,
interrogate him, and conclude the session by implanting the
suggestion that when he emerges from trance he will not
remember anything about what has happened."
Although the CIA's hypnosis work had advanced considerably by
the early 1960s, you wouldn't know it from reading Deshere's
report for Studies in Intelligence. At the same time, Deshere does
have plenty to say about potential roles for hypnosis in the spy
trade, exploring several crucial questions about the utility of the
technique. Can interrogatees under trance be made to tell the truth
and nothing but the truth? Can they be hypnotized without their
quiescence or their knowledge? Can they, though post-hypnotic
suggestion, be turned into virtual spy-robots to do the CIA's
bidding? Can amnesia be induced by the hypno-handlers to erase
memories of spy missions?
After conducting a lengthy analysis, Deshere concluded that there
was probably some use for hypnosis in interrogations, of a very
limited nature. He wrote that "the hypnotic situation, rather than

hypnosis itself, could be used to relieve a person of any sense of guilt for his behavior, giving him the notion that he is helpless to prevent his manipulation by the interrogator." Deshere described how such an operation could work:

"A captive's anxiety could be heightened, for example, by rumors that the interrogator possesses semi-magical techniques of extracting information. A group of collaborating captives could verify that interrogees lose all control over their actions, and so on. After such preliminary conditioning, a 'trance' could be induced with drugs in a setting described by Orne [the MKULTRA researcher discussed above] as the 'magic room,' where a number of devices could be used to convince the subject that he is responding to suggestions."

Once the interrogatee was persuaded that he was under the control of his handlers, Deshere reasoned, "the individual could legitimately renounce responsibility for divulging information, much as if he had done it in delirium."

Deshere's elaborate plan was pretty dry stuff, when compared to some of the more grandiose CIA hypnosis schemes hatched during the early years of the Cold War. Just how far did the CIA take its investigation of the uses of hypnosis? We may never know all of the answers, but this once-secret report offers more clues as to why the trance technique was added to the CIA's arsenal of mindcontrol weapons.

CENTRAL INTELLIGENCE AGENCY
WASHINGTON 25, D. C.

OFFICE OF THE DIRECTOR

25 APR 1956

MEMORANDUM FOR: The Honorable J. Edgar Hoover
Director, Federal Bureau of Investigation

SUBJECT: Brainwashing

The attached study on brainwashing was prepared by my staff in response to the increasing acute interest in the subject throughout the intelligence and security components of the Government. I feel you will find it well worth your personal attention. It represents the thinking of leading psychologists, psychiatrists and intelligence specialists, based in turn on interviews with many individuals who have had personal experience with Communist brainwashing, and on extensive research and testing. While individuals specialists hold divergent views on various aspects of this most complex subject, I believe the study reflects a synthesis of majority expert opinion. I will, of course, appreciate any comments on it that you or your staff may have.

(signed)
Allen W. Dulles
Director

ENCLOSURE

A REPORT ON COMMUNIST BRAINWASHING

The report that follows is a condensation of a study by training experts of the important classified and unclassified information available on this subject.

BACKGROUND

Brainwashing, as a technique, has been used for centuries and is no mystery to psychologists. In this sense, brainwashing means involuntary reeducation of basic beliefs and values. All people are being reeducated continually. New information changes one's beliefs. Everyone has experienced to some degree the conflict that ensues when new information is not consistent with prior belief. The experience of the brainwashed individual differs in that the inconsistent information is forced upon the individual under controlled conditions after the possibility of critical judgment has been removed by a variety of methods.

There is no question that an individual can be broken psychologically by captors with knowledge and willingness to persist in techniques aimed at deliberately destroying the integration of a personality. Although it is probable that everyone reduced to such a confused, disoriented state will respond to the introduction of new beliefs, this cannot be stated dogmatically.

PRINCIPLES OF HUMAN CONTROL AND REACTION TO CONTROL

There are progressive steps in exercising control over an individual and changing his behaviour and personality integration. The following five steps are typical of behaviour changes in any controlled individual:

1. Making the individual aware of control is the first stage in changing his behaviour. A small child is made aware of the physical and psychological control of his parents and quickly recognizes that an overwhelming force must be reckoned with. So, a controlled adult comes to recognize the overwhelming powers of the state and the impersonal, "incarcerative" machinery in which he is enmeshed. The individual recognizes that definite limits have been put upon the ways he can respond.

(Approved for Release) (62-80750-2712X)
(Date: 8 FEB 1984)

2. Realization of his complete dependence upon the controlling system is a major factor in the controlling of his behavior. The controlled adult is forced to accept the fact that food, tobacco, praise, and the only social contact that he will get come from the very interrogator who exercises control over him.
3. The awareness of control and recognition of dependence result in causing internal conflict and breakdown of previous patterns of behaviour. Although this transition can be relatively mild in the case of a child, it is almost invariably severe for the adult undergoing brainwashing. Only an individual who holds his values lightly can change them easily. Since the brainwasher-interrogators aim to have the individuals

undergo profound emotional change, they force their victims to seek out painfully what is desired by the controlling individual. During this period the victim is likely to have a mental breakdown characterized by delusions and hallucinations.

4. Discovery that there is an acceptable solution to his problem is the first stage of reducing the individual's conflict. It is characteristically reported by victims of brainwashing that this discovery led to an overwhelming feeling of relief that the horror of internal conflict would cease and that perhaps they would not, after all, be driven insane. It is at this point that they are prepared to make major changes in their value-system. This is an automatic rather than voluntary choice. They have lost their ability to be critical.

5. Reintergration of values and identification with the controlling system is the final stage in changing the behaviour of the controlled individual. A child who has learned a new, socially desirable behaviour demonstrates its importance by attempting to as—apt the new behaviour to a variety of other situations. Similar states in the brainwashed adult are

(SECTION DELETED BY CIA)

pitiful. His new value-system, his manner of perceiving, organizing, and giving meaning to events, is virtually independent of his former value—system. He is no longer capable of thinking or speaking in concepts other than those he has adopted. He tends to identify by expressing thanks to his captors for helping him see the light. Brainwashing can be achieved without using illegal means. Anyone willing to use known principles of control and reactions to control and capable of demonstrating the patience needed in raising a child can probably achieve successful brainwashing.

COMMUNIST CONTROL TECHNIQUES AND THEIR EFFECTS

A description of usual communist control techniques follows.

1. Interrogation. There are at least two ways in which "interrogation" is used:

   a. Elicitation, which is designed to get the individual to surrender protected information, is a form of interrogation. One major difference between elicitation and interrogation used to achieve brainwashing is that the mind of the individual must be kept clear to permit coherent, undistorted disclosure of protected information.

   b. Elicitation for the purpose of brainwashing consists of questioning, argument, indoctrination, threats, cajolery, praise, hostility, and a variety of other pressures. The aim of this interrogation is to hasten the breakdown of the individual's value system and to encourage the substitution of a different value-system. The procurement of protected information is secondary and is used as a device to increase pressure upon the individual. The term "interrogation" in this paper will refer, in general, to this type. The "interrogator" is the individual who conducts this type of interrogation and who controls the administration of the other pressures. He is the protagonist against whom the victim develops his conflict, and upon whom the victim develops a state of dependency as he seeks some solution to his conflict.

2. Physical Torture and Threats of Torture. Two types of physical torture are distinguishable more by their psychological effect in inducing conflict than by the degree of painfulness:

   a. The first type is one in which the victim has a passive role in the pain inflicted on him (e.g., beatings). His conflict involves the decision of whether or not to give in to demands in order to avoid further pain. Generally, brutality of this type was not found to achieve the desired results. Threats of torture were found more effective, as fear of pain causes greater conflict within the individual than does pain itself.

   b. The second type of torture is represented by requiring the individual to stand in one spot for several hours or assume some other pain-inducing position. Such a requirement often engenders in the individual a determination to "stick it out." This internal act of resistance provide a feeling of moral superiority at first. As time passes and his pain mounts, however, the individual becomes aware that it is his own original determination to resist that is causing the continuance of pain. A conflict develops within the individual between his moral determination and his desire to collapse and discontinue the pain. It is this extra internal conflict, in addition to the conflict over whether or not to give in to the demands made of him, that tends to make this method of torture more effective in the breakdown of the individual personality.

3. Isolation. Individual differences in reaction to isolation are probably greater than to any other method. Some individuals appear to be able to withstand prolonged periods of isolation without deleterious effects, while a relatively short period of isolation reduces others to the verge of psychosis. Reaction varies with the conditions of the isolation cell. Some sources have indicated a strong reaction to filth and vermin, although they had negligible reactions to the isolation. Others reacted violently to isolation in relatively clean cells. The predominant cause of breakdown in such situations is a lack of sensory stimulation (i.e., grayness of walls, lack of sound, absence of social contact, etc.). Experimental subjects exposed to this condition have reported vivid hallucinations and overwhelming fears of losing their sanity.

4. Control of Communication. This is one of the most effective methods for creating a sense of helplessness and despair. This measure might well be considered the

cornerstone of the communist system of control. It consists of strict regulation of the mail, reading materials, broadcast materials, and social contact available to the individual. The need to communicate is so great that when the usual channels are blocked, the individual will resort to any open channel, almost regardless of the implications of using that particular channel. Many POWs in Korea, whose only act of "collaboration" was to sign petitions and "peace appeals," defended their actions on the ground that this was the only method of letting the outside world know they were still alive. May stated that their morale and fortitude would have been increased immeasurably had leaflets of encouragement been dropped to them. When the only contact with the outside world is via the interrogator, the prisoner comes to develop extreme dependency on his interrogator and hence loses another prop to his morale.

Another wrinkle in communication control is the informer system. The recruitment of informers in POW camps discouraged communication between inmates. POWs who feared that every act or thought of resistance would be communicated to the camp administrators, lost faith in their fellow man and were forced to "untrusting individualism." Informers are also under several stages of brainwashing and elicitation to develop and maintain control over the victims.

5. Induction of Fatigue. This is a well-known device for breaking will power and critical powers of judgment. Deprivation of sleep results in more intense psychological debilitation than does any other method of engendering fatigue. The communists vary their methods. "Conveyor belt" interrogation that last 50-60 hours will make almost any individual compromise, but there is danger that this will kill the victim. It is safer to conduct interrogations of 8-10 hours at night while forcing the prisoner to remain awake during the day. Additional interruptions in the remaining 2-3 hours of allotted sleep quickly reduce the most resilient individual. Alternate administration of drug stimulants and depressants hastens the process of fatigue and sharpens the psychological reactions of excitement and depression.

Fatigue, in addition to reducing the will to resist, also produces irritation and fear that arise from increased "slips of the tongue," forgetfulness, and decreased ability to maintain orderly thought processes.

6. Control of Food, Water and Tobacco. The controlled individual is made intensely aware of his dependence upon his interrogator for the quality and quantity of his food and tobacco. The exercise of this control usually follows a pattern. No food and little or no water is permitted the individual for several days prior to interrogation. When the prisoner first complains of this to the interrogator, the latter expresses surprise at such inhumane treatment. He makes a demand of the prisoner. If the latter complies, he receives a good meal. If he does not, he gets a diet of unappetizing food containing limited vitamins, minerals, and calories. This diet is supplemented occasionally by the interrogator if the prisoner "cooperates." Studies of controlled starvation indicate that the whole value-system of the subjects underwent a change. Their irritation increased as their ability to think clearly

decreased. The control of tobacco presented an even greater source of conflict for heavy smokers. Because tobacco is not necessary to life, being manipulated by his craving for it can in the individual a strong sense of guilt.

7. Criticism and Self-Criticism. There are mechanisms of communist thought control. Self-criticism gains its effectiveness from the fact that although it is not a crime for a man to be wrong, it is a major crime to be stubborn and to refuse to learn. Many individuals feel intensely relieved in being able to share their sense of guilt. Those individuals however, who have adjusted to handling their guilt internally have difficulty adapting to criticism and self-criticism. In brainwashing, after a sufficient sense of guilt has been created in the individual, sharing and self-criticism permit relief. The price paid for this relief, however, is loss of individuality and increased dependency.

8. Hypnosis and Drugs as Controls. There is no reliable evidence that the communists are making widespread use of drugs or hypnosis in brainwashing or elicitation. The exception to this is the use of common stimulants or depressants in inducing fatigue and "mood swings."

9. Other methods of control, which when used in conjunction with the basic processes, hasten the deterioration of prisoners' sense of values and resistance are:

   a. Requiring a case history or autobiography of the prisoner provides a mine of information for the interrogator in establishing and "documenting" accusations.

   b. Friendliness of the interrogator, when least expected, upsets the prisoner's ability to maintain a critical attitude.

   c. Petty demands, such as severely limiting the allotted time for use of toilet facilities or requiring the POW to kill hundreds of flies, are harassment methods.

   d. Prisoners are often humiliated by refusing them the use of toilet facilities during interrogation until they soil themselves. Often prisoners were not permitted to bathe for weeks until they felt contemptible.

   e. Conviction as a war criminal appears to be a potent factor in creating despair in the individual. One official analysis of the pressures exerted by the ChiComs on "confessors" and "non-confessors" to participation in bacteriological warfare in Korea showed that actual trial and conviction of "war crimes" was overwhelmingly associated with breakdown and confession.

   f. Attempted elicitation of protected information at various times during the brainwashing process diverted the individual from awareness of the deterioration of his value-system. The fact that, in most cases, the ChiComs did not want or need such intelligence was not known to the prisoner. His attempts to protect such information was made at the expense of hastening his own breakdown.

THE EXERCISE OF CONTROL: A "SCHEDULE" FOR BRAINWASHING

From the many fragmentary accounts reviewed, the following appears to be the most likely description of what occurs during brainwashing.

In the period immediately following capture, the captors are faced with the problem of deciding on best ways of exploitation of the prisoners. Therefore, early treatment is similar both for those who are to be exploited through elicitation and those who are to undergo brainwashing. concurrently with being interrogated and required to write a detailed personal history, the prisoner undergoes a physical and psychological "softening-up" which includes: limited unpalatable food rations, withholding of tobacco, possible work details, severely inadequate use of toilet facilities, no use of facilities for personal cleanliness, limitation of sleep such as requiring a subject to sleep with a bright light in his eyes. Apparently the interrogation and autobiographical material, the reports of the prisoner's behaviour in confinement, and tentative "personality typing" by the interrogators, provide the basis upon which exploitation plans are made.

There is a major difference between preparation for elicitation and for brainwashing. Prisoners exploited through elicitation must retain sufficient clarity of thought to be able to give coherent, factual accounts. In brainwashing, on the other hand, the first thing attacked is clarity of thought. To develop a strategy of defense, the controlled individual must determine what plans have been made for his exploitation. Perhaps the best cues he can get are internal reactions to the pressures he undergoes.

The most important aspect of the brainwashing process is the interrogation. The other pressures are designed primarily to help the interrogator achieve his goals. The following states are created systematically within the individual. These may vary in order, but all are necessary to the brainwashing process:

1. A feeling of helplessness in attempting to deal with the impersonal machinery of control.
2. An initial reaction of "surprise."
3. A feeling of uncertainty about what is required of him.
4. A developing feeling of dependence upon the interrogator.
5. A sense of doubt and loss of objectivity.
6. Feelings of guilt.
7. A questioning attitude toward his own value-system.
8. A feeling of potential "breakdown," i.e., that he might go crazy.
9. A need to defend his acquired principles.
10. A final sense of "belonging" (identification).

A feeling of helplessness in the face of the impersonal machinery of control is carefully engendered within the prisoner. The individual who receives the preliminary treatment described above not only begins to feel like an "animal" but also feels that nothing can be done about it. No one pays any personal attention to him. His complaints fall on deaf ears. His loss of communication, if he has been isolated, creates a feeling that he has been "forgotten." Everything that happens to him occurs according to an impersonal; time schedule that has nothing to do with his needs. The voices and footsteps of the guards are muted. He notes many contrasts, e.g., his greasy, unpalatable food may be served on battered tin dishes by guards immaculately dressed in white. The first steps in "depersonalization" of the prisoner have begun. He has no idea what to expect. Ample opportunity is allotted for him to ruminate upon all the unpleasant or painful things that could happen to him. He approaches the main interrogator with mixed feelings of relief and fright.

Surprise is commonly used in the brainwashing process. The prisoner is rarely prepared for the fact that the interrogators are usually friendly and considerate at first. They make every effort to demonstrate that they are reasonable human beings. Often they apologize for bad treatment received by the prisoner and promise to improve his lot if he, too, is reasonable. This behaviour is not what he has steeled himself for. He lets down some of his defenses and tries to take a reasonable attitude. The first occasion he balks at satisfying a request of the interrogator, however, he is in for another surprise. The formerly reasonable interrogator unexpectedly turns into a furious maniac. The interrogator is likely to slap the prisoner or draw his pistol and threaten to shoot him. Usually this storm of emotion ceases as suddenly as it began and the interrogator stalks from the room. These surprising changes create doubt in the prisoner as to his very ability to perceive another person's motivations correctly. His next interrogation probably will be marked by impassivity in the interrogator's mien.

A feeling of uncertainty about what is required of him is likewise carefully engendered within the individual. Pleas of the prisoner to learn specifically of what he is accused and by whom are side-stepped by the interrogator. Instead, the prisoner is asked to tell why he thinks he is held and what he feels he is guilty of. If the prisoner fails to come up with anything, he is accused in terms of broad generalities (e.g., espionage, sabotage, acts of treason against the "people"). This usually provokes the prisoner to make some statement about his activities. If this takes the form of a denial, he is usually sent to isolation on further decreased food rations to "think over" his crimes. This process can be repeated again and again. As soon as the prisoner can think of something that might be considered self-incriminating, the interrogator appears momentarily satisfied. The prisoner is asked to write down his statement in his own words and sign it.

Meanwhile a strong sense of dependence upon the interrogator is developed. It does not take long for the prisoner to realize that the interrogator is the source of all punishment, all gratification, and all communication. The interrogator, meanwhile, demonstrates his unpredictability. He is perceived by the prisoner as a creature of whim. At times, the interrogator can be pleased very easily and at other times no effort on the part of the prisoner will placate him. The prisoner may begin to channel so much energy into trying to predict the behaviour of the unpredictable interrogator that he loses track of what is happening inside himself.

After the prisoner has developed the above psychological and emotional reactions to a sufficient degree, the brainwashing begins in earnest. First, the prisoner's remaining critical faculties must be destroyed. He undergoes long, fatiguing interrogations while looking at a bright light. He is called back again and again for interrogations after minimal sleep. He may undergo torture that tends to create internal conflict. Drugs may be used to accentuate his "mood swings." He develops depression when the interrogator is being kind and becomes euphoric when the interrogator is threatening the direst penalties. Then the cycle is reversed. The prisoner finds himself in a constant state of anxiety which prevents him from relaxing even when he is permitted to sleep. Short periods of isolation now bring on visual and auditory hallucinations. The prisoner feels himself losing his objectivity. It is in this state that the prisoner must keep up an endless argument with the interrogator. He may be faced with the confessions of other individuals who "collaborated" with him in his crimes. The prisoner seriously begins to doubts his own memory. This feeling is heightened by his inability to recall little things like the names of the people he knows very well or the date of his birth. The interrogator patiently sharpens this feeling of doubt by more questioning. This tends to create a serious state of uncertainty when the individual has lost most of his critical faculties.

The prisoner must undergo additional internal conflict when strong feelings of guilt are aroused within him. As any clinical psychologist is aware, it is not at all difficult to create such feelings. Military servicemen are particularly vulnerable. No one can morally justify killing even in wartime. The usual justification is on the grounds of necessity or self-defense. The interrogator is careful to circumvent such justification. He keeps the interrogation directed toward the prisoner's moral code. Every moral vulnerability is exploited by incessant questioning along this line until the prisoner begins to question the very fundamentals of his own value-system. The prisoner must constantly fight a potential breakdown. He finds that his mind is "going blank" for longer and longer periods of time. He can not think constructively. If he is to maintain any semblance of psychological integrity, he must bring to an end this state of interminable internal conflict. He signifies a willingness to write a confession.

If this were truly the end, no brainwashing would have occurred. The individual would simply have given in to intolerable pressure. Actually, the final stage of the brainwashing process has just begun. No matter what the prisoner writes in his confession the interrogator is not satisfied. The interrogator questions every sentence of the confession. He begins to edit it with the prisoner. The prisoner is forced to argue against every change. This is the essence of brainwashing. Every time that he gives in on a point to the interrogator, he must rewrite his whole confession. Still the interrogator is not satisfied. In a desperate attempt to maintain some semblance of integrity and to avoid further brainwashing, the prisoner must begin to argue that what he has already confessed to is true. He begins to accept as his own the statements he has written. He uses many of the interrogator's earlier arguments to buttress his position. By this process, identification with the interrogator's value-system becomes complete. It is extremely important to recognize that a qualitative change has taken place within the prisoner. The brainwashed victim does not consciously change his value-system; rather the change occurs despite his efforts. He is no more responsible for this change than is an individual who "snaps" and becomes psychotic. And like the psychotic, the prisoner is not even aware of the transition.

DEFENSIVE MEASURES OTHER THAN ON THE POLICY AND PLANNING LEVEL

1. Training of Individuals potentially subject to communist control.

    Training should provide for the trainee a realistic appraisal of what control pressures the communists are likely to exert and what the usual human reactions are to such pressures. The trainee must learn the most effective ways of combatting his own reactions to such pressures and he must learn reasonable expectations as to what his behaviour should be. Training has two decidedly positive effects; first, it provides the trainee with ways of combatting control; second, it provides the basis for developing an immeasurable boost in morale. Any positive action that the individual can take, even if it is only slightly effective, gives him a sense of control over a situation that is otherwise controlling him.

2. Training must provide the individual with the means of recognizing realistic goals for himself.

    a. Delay in yielding may be the only achievement that can be hoped for. In any particular operation, the agent needs the support of knowing specifically how long he must hold out to save an operation, protect his cohorts, or gain some other goal.

    b. The individual should be taught how to achieve the most favorable treatment and how to behave and make necessary concessions to obtain minimum penalties.

    c. Individual behavioural responses to the various communist control pressures differ markedly. Therefore, each trainee should know his own particular assets and limitations in resisting specific pressures. He can learn these only under laboratory conditions simulating the actual pressures he may have to face.

    d. Training must provide knowledge of the goals and the restrictions placed upon his communist interrogator. The trainee should know what controls are on his interrogator and to what extent he can manipulate the interrogator. For example, the interrogator is not permitted to fail to gain "something" from the controlled individual. The knowledge that, after the victim has proved that he is a "tough nut to crack" he can sometimes indicate that he might compromise on some little point to help the interrogator in return for more favorable treatment, may be useful indeed. Above all, the potential victim of communist control can gain a great deal of psychological support from the knowledge that the communist interrogator is not a completely free agent who can do whatever he wills with his victim.

e. The trainee must learn what practical cues might aid him in recognizing the specific goals of his interrogator. The strategy of defense against elicitation may differ markedly from the strategy to prevent brainwashing. To prevent elicitation, the individual may hasten his own state of mental confusion; whereas, to prevent brainwashing, maintaining clarity of thought processes is imperative.

f. The trainee should obtain knowledge about communist "carrots" as well as "sticks." The communists keep certain of their promises and always renege on others. For example, the demonstrable fact that "informers" receive no better treatment than other prisoners should do much to prevent this particular evil. On the other hand, certain meaningless concessions will often get a prisoner a good meal.

g. In particular, it should be emphasized to the trainee that, although little can be done to control the pressures exerted upon him, he can learn something about controlling his personal reactions to specific pressures. The trainee can gain much from learning something about internal conflict and conflict-producing mechanisms. He should learn to recognize when someone is trying to arouse guilt feelings and what behavioural reactions can occur as a response to guilt.

h. Finally, the training must teach some methods that can be utilized in thwarting particular communist control techniques:

Elicitation. In general, individuals who are the hardest to interrogate for information are those who have experienced previous interrogations. Practice in being the victim of interrogation is a sound training device.

Torture. The trainee should learn something about the principles of pain and shock. There is a maximum to the amount of pain that can actually be felt. Any amount of pain can be tolerated for a limited period of time. In addition, the trainee can be fortified by the knowledge that there are legal limitations upon the amount of torture that can be inflicted by communist jailers.

Isolation. The psychological effects of isolation can probably be thwarted best by mental gymnastics and systematic efforts on the part of the isolate to obtain stimulation for his neural end organs.

Controls on Food and Tobacco. Foods given by the communists will always be enough to maintain survival. Sometimes the victim gets unexpected opportunities to supplement his diet with special minerals, vitamins and other nutrients (e.g., "iron" from the rust of prison bars). In some instances, experience has shown that individuals could exploit refusal to eat. Such refusal usually resulted in the transfer of the individual to a hospital where he received vitamin injections and nutritious food. Evidently attempts of this kind to commit suicide arouse the greatest concern in communist officials. If deprivation of tobacco is the control being exerted, the victim can gain moral satisfaction from "giving up" tobacco. He can't lose since he is not likely to get any anyway.

Fatigue. The trainee should learn reactions to fatigue and how to overcome them insofar as possible. For example, mild physical exercise "clears the head" in a fatigue state.

Writing Personal Accounts and Self-Criticism. Experience has indicated that one of the most effective ways of combatting these pressures is to enter into the spirit with an overabundance of enthusiasm. Endless written accounts of inconsequential material have virtually "smothered" some eager interrogators. In the same spirit, sober, detailed self-criticisms of the most minute "sins" has sometimes brought good results.

Guidance as to the priority of positions he should defend. Perfectly compatible responsibilities in the normal execution of an individual's duties may become mutually incompatible in this situation. Take the example of a senior grade military officer. He has the knowledge of sensitive strategic intelligence which it is his duty to protect. He has the responsibility of maintaining the physical fitness of his men and serving as a model example for their behaviour. The officer may go to the camp commandant to protest the treatment of the POWs and the commandant assures him that treatment could be improved if he will swap something for it. Thus to satisfy one responsibility he must compromise another. The officer, in short, is in a constant state of internal conflict. But if the officer is given the relative priority of his different responsibilities, he is supported by the knowledge that he won't be held accountable for any other behaviour if he does his utmost to carry out his highest priority responsibility. There is considerable evidence that many individuals tried to evaluate the priority of their responsibilities on their own, but were in conflict over whether others would subsequently accept their evaluations. More than one individual was probably brainwashed while he was trying to protect himself against elicitation.

CONCLUSIONS

The application of known psychological principles can lead to an understanding of brainwashing.

1. There is nothing mysterious about personality changes resulting from the brainwashing process.
2. Brainwashing is a complex process. Principles of motivation, perception, learning, and physiological deprivation are needed to account for the results achieved in brainwashing.
3. Brainwashing is an involuntary reeducation of the fundamental beliefs of the individual. To attack the problem successfully, the brainwashing process must be differentiated clearly from general education methods for thought-control or mass indoctrination, and elicitation.
4. It appears possible for the individual, through training, to develop limited defensive techniques against brainwashing. Such defensive measures are likely to be most effective if directed toward thwarting individual emotional reactions to brainwashing techniques rather than toward thwarting the techniques themselves.

15 August 1955

—

(note Declassified)

SECRET

CENTRAL INTELLIGENCE AGENCY WASHINGTON 25, D. C.

19 JUN 1964

(Commission No. 1131)

MEMORANDUM FOR: Mr. J. Lee Rankin
General Counsel
President's Commission on the Assassination of President Kennedy

SUBJECT: Soviet Brainwashing Techniques

1. Reference is made to your memorandum of 19 May 1964, requesting that materials relative to Soviet techniques in mind conditioning and brainwashing be made available to the Commission.
2. At my request, experts on these subjects within the CIA have prepared a brief survey of Soviet research in the direction and control of human behavior, a copy of which

is attached. The Commission may retain this document. Please note that the use of certain sensitive materials requires that a sensitivity indicator be affixed.

3. In the immediate future, this Agency will make available to you a collection of overt and classified materials on these subjects, which the Commission may retain.

4. I hope that these documents will be responsive to the Commission's needs.

(SIGNED)

(DECLASSIFIED) Richard Helms
(By C.I.A.) Deputy Director for Plans
(letter of _____)
(_____)

Attachment

CD 1131 SECRET

MEMORANDUM

SUBJECT: Soviet Research and Development in the Field of Direction and Control of Human Behavior.

1. There are two major methods of altering or controlling human behavior, and the Soviets are interested in both. The first is psychological; the second, pharmacological. The two may be used as individual methods or for mutual reinforcement. For long-term control of large numbers of people, the former method is more promising than the latter. In dealing with individuals, the U.S. experience suggests the pharmacological approach (assisted by psychological techniques) would be the only effective method. Neither method would be very effective for single individuals on a long term basis.

2. Soviet research on the pharmacological agents producing behavioral effects has consistently lagged about five years behind Western research. They have been interested in such research, however, and are now pursuing research on such chemicals as LSD-25, amphetamines, tranquillizers, hypnotics, and similar materials. There is no present evidence that the Soviets have any singular, new, potent drugs to force a course of action on an individual. They are aware, however, of the tremendous drive produced by drug addiction, and PERHAPS could couple this with psychological direction to achieve control of an individual.

3. The psychological aspects of behavior control would include not only conditioning by repetition and training, but such things as hypnosis, deprivation, isolation,

manipulation of guilt feelings, subtle or overt threats, social pressure, and so on. Some of the newer trends in the USSR are as follows:

a. The adoption of a multidisciplinary approach integrating biological, social and physical-mathematical research in attempts better to understand, and eventually, to control human behavior in a manner consonant with national plans.
b. The outstanding feature, in addition to the interdisciplinary approach, is a new concern for mathematical approaches to an understanding of behavior. Particularly notable are attempts to use modern information theory, automata theory, and feedback concepts in interpreting the mechanisms by which the "second signal system," i.e., speech and associated phenomena, affect human behavior. Implied by this "second signal system," using INFORMATION inputs as causative agents rather than chemical agents, electrodes or other more exotic techniques applicable, perhaps, to individuals rather than groups.
c. This new trend, observed in the early Post-Stalin Period, continues. By 1960 the word "cybernetics" was used by the Soviets to designate this new trend. This new science is considered by some as the key to understanding the human brain and the product of its functioning—psychic activity and personality—to the development of means for controlling it and to ways for molding the character of the "New Communist Man." As one Soviet author puts it: Cybernetics can be used in "molding of a child's character, the inculcation of knowledge and techniques, the amassing of experience, the establishment of social behavior patterns . . . all functions which can be summarized as 'control' of the growth process of the individual." 1/Students of particular disciplines in the USSR, such as psychologist and social scientists, also support the general cybernetic trend. 2/ (Blanked by CIA)

4. In summary, therefore, there is no evidence that the Soviets have any techniques or agents capable of producing particular behavioral patterns which are not available in the West. Current research indicates that the Soviets are attempting to develop a technology for controlling the development of behavioral patterns among the citizenry of the USSR in accordance with politically determined requirements of the system. Furthermore, the same technology can be applied to more sophisticated approaches to the "coding" of information for transmittal to population targets in the "battle for the minds of men." Some of the more esoteric techniques such as ESP or, as the Soviets call it, "biological radio-communication," and psychogenic agents such as LSD, are receiving some overt attention with, possibly, applications in mind for individual behavior control under clandestine conditions. However, we require more information than is currently available in order to establish or disprove planned or actual applications of various methodologies by Soviet scientists to the control of actions of particular individuals.

References

1. Itelson, Lev, "Pedagogy: An Exact Science?" *USSR* October 1963, p. 10.
2. Borzek, Joseph, "Recent Developments in Soviet Psychology," *Annual Review of Psychology*, vol. 15, 1964, p. 493-594.

The first letter and attachment are from DECLASSIFIED DOCUMENTS 1984 microfilms under MKULTRA (84) 002258, published by Research Publication Woodbridge, CT 06525. Some original markings were not retyped, but the content is the same.

The second letter and attachment are from the Warren Commission documents. Notice should be paid to the different tone Helms gives to his letter, keeping in mind he was found guilty of lying to Congress. He places greater emphasis on "Soviet" practices and tries to diminish breakthroughs gained by Americans. Some thought should be given as to WHY the Warren Commission sought such documents (remembering that ALLEN DULLES was a member of that Commission). They were exploring the Manchurian candidate theory. It was revealed during the Church Committee hearings of 1975 that Helms had been in charge of Project AMLASH, a program to assassinate Castro (Cuba), Trujillo (Dominican Republic), Diem (RVN), Schneider (Chile) using MAFIA figures John Roselli and Santos Trafficante to do the job.

Care was used to insure lines appear in same length and order. Page length will have to be adjusted if you desire to print this. Look for other specials soon. David John Moses.

APPENDIX 2

Glossary of Common NLP Terms

Our primary goal is to provide you with reference experiences for the attitudes that characterize the NLP way of perceiving reality and for the trail of techniques that have been generated as a consequence. Since many people desire a map (no matter how vague) of the territory before proceeding with their journey, we also offer this glossary of terms. We trust that you understand that dictionary definitions are, of necessity, "circular" and are most useful when they direct you to the reference experiences.

Accessing Cues—Behaviors that are correlated with the use of a particular representational system; i.e., eye movements, postures, breathing, etc.

Analog Change—A change which varies continuously; e.g., a dimmer control for lights or a shift in body position.

Analog Marking—Emphasizing a part of a sentence using verbal or nonverbal means; e.g., a louder tone or a hand gesture.

Anchor—A trigger that leads to an experience as fully and completely as possible (with all the senses); looking out from one's own eyes.

Auditory—Referring to the sense of hearing.

Backtrack—To review or summarize.

Break State—To change a person's state dramatically.

Behavioral Flexibility—The ability to vary one's behavior in order to elicit a response from another person.

Calibrate—To "read" another person's verbal and nonverbal responses and associate specific behaviors with specific internal processes or states.

Calibrated Loop—An ongoing interaction in which specific behaviors of each person trigger specific responses in the other.

Chaining Anchors—Firing anchors sequentially in order to direct a person's experience along that sequence.

Channel—One of the five senses or representational systems.

Chunk Size—The size of the object, situation, or experience being considered. This can be altered by chunking up (a broader focus), chunking down (a more specific focus), or chunking sideways or laterally (focusing on others of the same type of class). For example, beginning with a car, "chunking down" might be to a Ford, "chunking up" might be to a means of transportation, and "chunking sideways" might be to a plane or train.

Collapsing Anchors—Firing anchors simultaneously in order to promote integration of the experiences.

Complex Equivalent—A linguistic term to describe the complex set of behaviors that equal a certain nominalization in a person's map of reality; e.g., the behaviors that are "proof" that a certain person "loves" you.

Congruent—When all of a person's internal strategies, behaviors, and parts are in agreement and working together.

Contrastive Analysis—To determine the differences between the submodalities of two or more representations.

Conversational Postulates—Behavioral presuppositions which are part of the culture and language patterns but are not identified overtly; e.g., "Do you have a watch?" leads the other person to tell you the time.

Critical Submodalities—The submodalities which most determine a person's response.

Crossover Mirroring—Matching a person's rhythms but with a different type of behavior.

Deep Trance Identification—See second position.

Digital Change—A change which is all-or-none, on-or-off with no steps or positions in between the ends; e.g., a light is on or off, language.

Dissociated—Experiencing from a perspective other than your own.

Driver—The most crucial submodality so that changing it "automatically" changes many other submodalities.

Dovetail—To fit together more than one outcome, story, etc.

Ecology—Considering the effects on the whole system instead of on just one part or one person.

Embedded Command—Nesting a command so that it is grammatically not a command but is marked out as a command by your analogs; e.g., "It might be worthwhile considering how to *do that*!

Eye-Accessing Cues—Movements of a person's eyes that indicate the representational system being used.

Firing an Anchor—Repeating the overt behavior that triggers a certain response.

First Position—Experiencing the world from your own perspective or being associated into yourself.

Flexibility—Having more than one choice in a situation.

Future Pace—Rehearsing (mentally and physically) so that a specific behavior will occur naturally and automatically in a future situation.

Generative Intervention—An intervention that solves the presenting problem and also generates other changes that make the person's life better in many other ways.

Gustatory—Referring to the sense of taste.

Incongruent—When two or more of a person's parts or programs are in conflict.

Installation—Acquiring a new strategy or behavior.

Kinesthetic—Referring to the sense of feeling. May be subdivided into tactile feelings (Kt—physically feeling the outside world), proprioceptive feelings (Kp—internal body sensations such as muscle tension or relaxation), and meta feelings (Km—"emotional" responses about some object, situation or experience.)

Lead System—The representational system initially used to access stored information.

Leading—Guiding another person in a specific direction.

Lost Performative—A linguistic pattern in which the person performing the action or judgment is missing from the sentence.

Map of Reality—A person's perception of reality.

Mask—See perceptual filter.

Meta-model—A model of language patterns that focuses attention on words people use to delete, distort, generalize, limit, or specify their realities and also provides a series of outcome specification questions useful for recovering lost or unspecified information and or loosening rigid patterns of thinking.

Metaphor—Usually a story, parable, or analogy that relates one situation, experience or phenomenon to another.

Meta-Outcome—The outcome that is more general than the stated one; e.g., getting my self-respect back is the meta-outcome in "Killing that person will get my self-respect back." It is the "chunked up" outcome, so that killing that person becomes only one member of a class of behaviors that can be used to recover self-respect.

Meta-Person—Being in third positions.

Milton Model—A categorization of language patterns useful for delivering a message in such a way that the person readily accepts it.

Mirroring—Approximately matching one's behavior to that of another person.

Modal Operators—A linguistic term for the way one judges or evaluates actions; e.g., choice, possibility, impossibility, desire, necessity.

Modality—One of the five senses.

Modeling—Observing and specifying how something happens or how someone thinks or behaves, and then demonstrating the process for others.

Negative Command—A command that is marked out with analogs although it is grammatically stated in the negative; e.g., "Wouldn't that be a *good idea!*"

Nest—To fit one thing (outcome, story, etc.) within another.

Nominalization—A linguistic term for the words which result from the process of taking actions (verbs) and converting them into things (nouns) which actually have no existence as things; e.g., you can't put them in a wheelbarrow. Examples of nominalizations are "love," "freedom," "happiness," "respect," "frustration," etc. See complex equivalent.

Olfactory—Referring to the sense of smell.

Organ Language—Words that refer to specific body parts or activities; e.g., "Get off my back," "pain in the rear," etc.

Outcome—Desired goal or result.

Pacing—Matching or mirroring another person's verbal and/or nonverbal behavior. Useful for gaining short-term rapport.

Parts—Metaphoric representations of different facets of a person's strategies, programs, "personality" or ego states; e.g., the "parts" that want you to be safe, independent, in control, loved, respected, spiritual, etc. To be distinguished from the specific behaviors adopted by the "parts" to get their positive outcomes.

Perceptual Filter—An attitude, point of view, perspective or set of presuppositions about the object, person or situation. Also called a "mask."

Polarity Response—A response which reverses, negates, or takes the opposite position from the previous statement.

Predicates—Process words or words that express action or relationship with respect to a subject (verbs, adverbs and adjectives). The words may reflect the representational system being used or they may be nonspecific; e.g., "That looks good," "Sounds right to me," "That feels fine," or "I agree."

Preferred Representational System—The representational system which a person habitually uses to process information or experiences; usually the one in which the person can make the finest distinctions.

Process Words—See predicates.

Quotes—A method of expressing the desired message in quotations as if someone else said it.

Rapport—A condition in which trust, understanding, harmony, and cooperation has been established.

Reframing—A process by which a person's perception of a specific behavior is altered. Usually subdivided into context, meaning, and six-step reframing.

Remedial Intervention—An intervention that only solves the presenting problem.

Representational Systems—Referring to the five sense of seeing (visual), hearing (auditory), feeling (kinesthetic), tasting (gustatory), and smelling (olfactory).

Resource State—The experience of an ability, attitude, behavior, characteristic, perspective, or quality that is useful.

Second Position—Experiencing the world from the perspective of another person.

Secondary Gain—The positive or desired result (often hidden) of a seemingly undesired or problem behavior.

Sensory Acuity—The ability to use the senses to make distinctions between different bits of incoming information.

Sensory Based—Information which is correlated with what has been received by the five senses (as opposed to "Hallucinations").

Separator State—See break state.

Shift Referential Index—To take the perspective of someone else but to keep your own criteria.

Six-Step Reframe—A process in which an undesirable behavior is metaphorically separated from the desired outcome of the "part" so that the "part" can more easily adopt new behaviors that satisfy its positive intention and do not have the undesirable effects of the original behavior.

Sorting Polarities—Separating tendencies or "parts" that pull a person in opposite directions.

Stacking Anchors—Using the same anchor for a number of resources.

State—A state of being or a condition of body/mind or an experience at a particular moment.

Stealing an Anchor—Identifying an anchored sequence (stimulus-response) and then firing that anchor.

Stimulus-Response—The repeated association between an experience and a particular response; e.g., Pavlovian conditioning.

Strategy—A sequence of mental and behavioral steps which leads to a specific outcome; e.g., decision, learning, motivation, specific skills.

Submodalities—The subdivisions of the processing of the representational systems; e.g., visual information can be divided in black-and-white, color, 2-D, 3-D, bright, dim, clear, fuzzy, moving, still, large, small, etc.

Switch Referential Index—To take the perspective and the criteria of someone else.

Synthesia—An overlap between representational systems such as "see/feel" (feelings overlap with what is seen) or "hear/feel" (feelings overlap with what is heard).

Tag Questions—Negative questions tagged onto the end of a sentence in order to diffuse polarity responses; e.g., "Don't you?" "Can't you?" "Aren't you?" etc.

Tape Editing—A process of reviewing past behavior and then future pacing in order to alter future responses in similar situations.

Third Position—Experiencing the world from a distant position, outside all the persons in the interaction (as an "Observer," "Fair Witness," "Guardian Angel," etc.).

Transderivational Search—The process of searching back through one's memories to find a reference experience.

Translating—The process of rephrasing words from one representational system into another.

BIO

Dr. William Horton, Psy. D. was trained in crisis/hostage negotiation by the FBI at the FBI Academy in Quantico, Virginia. He is a licensed psychologist, an alcohol and drug counselor, and went through the Red Cross training for Critical Incident Stress Debriefing training. A veteran of the Army and Naval Reserve, Dr. Horton is considered one of the leading experts in subconscious communications. He has hypnotized over 100,000 people in his career! He has won more awards in the field of hypnosis than anyone in the last few years. He has lead trainings in hypnosis and NLP all over the world. His first book, *Primary Objective, Neuro-Linguistic Psychology and Guerrilla Warfare*, is being considered for a feature film. He has coauthored the best-selling *Selling Yourself to Others: the New Psychology of Sales*. He used these skills to overcome an injury and receive a black belt in three styles of karate. Join us and see why Dr. William Horton, Psy. D. was awarded the Rexford North Award, the highest award in the field of hypnosis. He has also won the 2001 Educator of the Year from the International Association of Counselors and Therapists and the highest award from the international Hypnosis Hall of Fame.

For Training in NLP, Hypnosis, and Mind Control Techniques contact Dr. Horton at (800) 758-4635 or email him at NFNLP@NFNLP.com